THE GREAT UPHEAVAL

D1829338

THE GREAT UPHEAVAL

MODERN ART FROM THE GUGGENHEIM COLLECTION

1910–1918

TRACEY BASHKOFF
MEGAN M. FONTANELLA

ESSAYS BY
TRACEY BASHKOFF
EMILY D. BILSKI
MILTON A. COHEN
MEGAN M. FONTANELLA
TARA WARD

GUGGENHEIM

THE GREAT UPHEAVAL

MODERN ART FROM THE GUGGENHEIM COLLECTION, 1910–1918

This exhibition is supported by a grant from the Joseph and Sylvia Slifka Foundation.

Published on the occasion of *The Great Upheaval: Modern Art from the Guggenheim Collection, 1910–1918*

Organized by Tracey Bashkoff and Megan M. Fontanella

Solomon R. Guggenheim Museum
February 4–June 1, 2011

© 2011 The Solomon R. Guggenheim Foundation, New York. All rights reserved

ISBN: 978-0-89207-415-0

Guggenheim Museum Publications
1071 Fifth Avenue
New York, NY 10128

Design: Jean Wilcox, Wilcox Design
Production: Jonathan Bowen, Melissa Secondino
Editorial: Kamilah Foreman, Stephen Hoban, Kara Mason

Cover: Juan Gris, *Newspaper and Fruit Dish* (*Journal et compotier*), March 1916 (detail, page 179)
Page 14: Franz Marc, *Broken Forms* (*Zerbrochene Formen*), 1914 (detail, page 171)

Printed in Iceland by Oddi

CONTENTS

THE SOLOMON R. GUGGENHEIM FOUNDATION

HONORARY TRUSTEES IN PERPETUITY

Solomon R. Guggenheim†
Justin K. Thannhauser†
Peggy Guggenheim†

HONORARY CHAIRMAN

Peter Lawson-Johnston

CHAIRMAN

William L. Mack

PRESIDENT

Jennifer Blei Stockman

VICE-PRESIDENTS

Wendy L-J. McNeil
Edward H. Meyer
Stephen C. Swid
Mark R. Walter

DIRECTOR

Richard Armstrong

TREASURER

Edward H. Meyer

SECRETARY

Edward F. Rover

DIRECTORS EMERITI

Thomas M. Messer
Thomas Krens

TRUSTEES

Jon Imanol Azua
Robert C. Baker
John Calicchio
Mary Sharp Cronson
Theodor Dalenson
Dimitris Daskalopoulos
Carl Gustaf Ehrnrooth
David Ganek
Peter Lawson-Johnston
Peter Lawson-Johnston II
Howard W. Lutnick
William L. Mack
Linda Macklowe
Wendy L-J. McNeil
Edward H. Meyer
Amy Phelan
Vladimir O. Potanin
Stephen M. Ross
Mortimer D. A. Sackler
Denise Saul
Michael P. Schulhof
James B. Sherwood
Jennifer Blei Stockman
Stephen C. Swid
John S. Wadsworth, Jr.
Mark R. Walter
John Wilmerding

HONORARY TRUSTEE

Hannelore B. Schulhof

TRUSTEES EMERITI

Robert M. Gardiner
Barbara Jonas
Samuel J. LeFrak†
Seymour Slive

TRUSTEES EX OFFICIO

Tiqui Atencio Demirdjian,
President, International Director's Council
John Leopoldo Fiorilla di Santa Croce,
Chairman, Executive Committee,
Peggy Guggenheim Collection Advisory Board

PREFACE

Certain historic moments crystallize in retrospect as particularly crucial, and *The Great Upheaval: Modern Art from the Guggenheim Collection, 1910–1918* argues that the years immediately prior to World War I through the end of the conflict were just such a period. The exhibition's title, taken from a text by Vasily Kandinsky, not only alludes to the revolutionary art that proliferated during the seminal prewar years, but also calls attention to the one hundredth anniversary of the formation of Der Blaue Reiter (The Blue Rider) in late 1911. Founded in Munich by Kandinsky and Franz Marc, two artists whose work the Guggenheim Museum has collected in-depth throughout its history, the group maintained a collaborative spirit of incorporating work by artists of diverse national origins and styles. Its subsequent disbandment eloquently symbolizes the hopes of a young generation shattered, literally and metaphorically, by the cataclysm of war. Intersections of politics and aesthetics remain of paramount interest to us today, and this exhibition follows on the illuminating *Chaos and Classicism: Art in France, Italy, and Germany, 1918–1936*, which the Guggenheim presented in late 2010 and early 2011.

While *The Great Upheaval* is far from uncharted territory for the museum, we arranged its presentation of more than one hundred paintings, sculptures, and works on paper chronologically, ascending the unique spiral of the building, designed by architect Frank Lloyd Wright, in order to trace the artistic development toward abstraction as well as emphasize the period's dynamic exchange of ideas across cultures and national boundaries. *The Great Upheaval* additionally offers us an institutional opportunity to celebrate masterpieces that have come to be regarded as signature works of our collection. Although the museum's founder, Solomon R. Guggenheim, is often associated with so-called nonobjective art, he enthusiastically collected representational works by Marc Chagall, Henri Rousseau, and others—as demonstrated here.

In this same spirit of exchange, the help of our various benefactors and supporters made it possible for us to assemble this beautiful exhibition from our esteemed collection. Particular acknowledgment must be given to Tracey Bashkoff, Curator of Collections and Exhibitions, and Megan M. Fontanella, Assistant Curator of Collections and Provenance, for their excellent and informed selection of works from our holdings, augmented by a number of important loans, for this exhibition and catalogue. The Peggy Guggenheim Collection, Venice, generously lent major works as well as Futurist masterpieces on extended loan to the institution from the Gianni Mattioli Collection in Milan. We are additionally grateful for the kindness of an individual who wishes to remain anonymous for lending significant works from a private collection. It is certainly with great pleasure that I acknowledge the Joseph and Sylvia Slifka Foundation, a strong supporter of collection programs at the museum, for its generous grant toward *The Great Upheaval*. I heartily commend this community of friends, colleagues, and vital constituents; without their generosity, we would not be able to bring this exhibition to fruition.

RICHARD ARMSTRONG
Director
Solomon R. Guggenheim Foundation and Museum

ACKNOWLEDGMENTS

Thanks to the foresight of the founders of the Solomon R. Guggenheim Foundation, New York, and the Peggy Guggenheim Collection, Venice, we are rich in our holdings of modern art and especially in the works of such pioneering artists as Constantin Brancusi, Marc Chagall, Robert Delaunay, Vasily Kandinsky, Fernand Léger, Kazimir Malevich, and Franz Marc. This publication, which follows the chronological organization of the accompanying exhibition, sheds light on the interactions and collaborations among members of the avant-garde during the pivotal years leading up to and including World War I. We are extremely grateful for the thoughtful contributions of our coauthors: Emily D. Bilski addresses the critical role of gallerist Heinrich Thannhauser in promoting modern art in Germany in 1911; Milton A. Cohen explores the extraordinary output of artist manifestos and writings in 1912, their philosophical significance, and their function in marketing modernist groups; and Tara Ward examines the phenomenon of simultaneity and the passage of time in both art and society in 1913. We thank Jean Wilcox for her inspired design of the book, which brilliantly captures the dynamism of this period.

At the Guggenheim Museum in New York, we are indebted to the numerous colleagues who have focused their expertise on this project's realization. We are particularly thankful for the sustained support of Richard Armstrong, Director, Solomon R. Guggenheim Foundation and Museum, and Nancy Spector, Deputy Director and Chief Curator, Solomon R. Guggenheim Foundation, as well as for the sound advice of our curatorial colleagues at the museum, including Susan Davidson, Senior Curator of Collections and Exhibitions; Vivien Greene, Curator of 19th- and Early 20th-Century Art; Karole Vail, Associate Curator; and Lauren Hinkson, Assistant Curator for Collections. We commend Andrew Chen, Curatorial Intern, and Flavia Frigeri, Hilla Rebay International Fellow, for tackling a variety of tasks with efficiency and good humor. Each of their contributions to the catalogue's timeline of events was especially invaluable. Yvette Crowley, Exhibitions Manager, carefully saw to the details of the presentation. Michele Heinrici, Registrar for Collections, deftly coordinated the logistical details of transportation and insurance with the help of Mark Schlemmer, Assistant Registrar for Collections, and under the leadership of MaryLouise Napier, Director of Registration. We are grateful to

Carol Stringari, Deputy Director and Chief Conservator, Solomon R. Guggenheim Foundation, and her exceptional Conservation Department staff for their passionate and thoughtful attention to our holdings. For their work on this project, we especially thank Gillian McMillan, Senior Conservator, Collections; Julie Barten, Conservator, Collections and Exhibitions; Nathan Otterson, Conservator, Objects; Jeffrey Warda, Associate Conservator, Paper; and Esther Chao, Assistant Conservator, Loans and Exhibitions. We are indebted to our colleagues at the Peggy Guggenheim Collection for assisting with myriad facets of the catalogue and exhibition: Chiara Barbieri, Director of Publications and Special Projects; Paul Schwarzbaum, Senior Technical Advisor and Conservator for Museum Construction and Overseas Exhibitions; Marco Rosin, Registrar; Grazina Subelyte, Registrar; and Simone Bottazzin, Publications Assistant.

We are fortunate to have had Melanie Taylor, Manager of Exhibition Design, as our partner in determining the look for this exhibition. We commend her for being endlessly creative while also sensitive to the architecture of the Frank Lloyd Wright–designed building. We likewise thank Marcia Fardella, Chief Graphic Designer, and Concetta Pereira, Production Supervisor, for their considerate approach to developing the exhibition's significant graphic presence. The preparation and installation of artworks was expertly supervised by David Bufano, Manager of Art Services and Preparations; Barry Hylton, Senior Exhibition Technician; and Paul Bridge and Derek Deluco, Exhibition Technicians. We acknowledge their enthusiastic team of art handlers and preparators, especially Jeffrey Clemens, Elisabeth Jaff, Colin O'Neil, and Christopher Williams. For their assistance in realizing the presentation in the galleries, we thank Michael Sarff, Exhibition Construction Manager; Peter B. Read, Manager of Exhibition Fabrications and Design; Mary Ann Hoag, Lighting Designer; and Peter Mallo, Chief Framemaker. Our appreciation goes to Mary Sharp Cronson, Founder and Producer, Works & Process, and Charles Fabius, Consulting Producer, at the museum.

The Guggenheim's outstanding Publications Department, led by Elizabeth Levy, Director of Publications and Web Site, worked tirelessly to accomplish the successful realization of this catalogue under the pressure of a rather tight deadline. We are appreciative of the hard work of the entire team, and especially Elizabeth Franzen, Associate Director of Publications, Editorial; Stephen Hoban, Managing Editor; Kamilah Foreman, Associate Editor; and Kara Mason, Assistant Editor. Melissa Secondino, Associate Director of Publications, Production, and Jonathan Bowen, Associate Production Manager, skillfully attended to design and production matters. David Heald, Director of Photographic Services and Chief Photographer, and Kristopher McKay, Assistant Photographer and Digital Imaging Specialist, have provided the reproductions for this catalogue. Francine Snyder, Manager of Library and Archives, assisted with archival materials for the presentation and catalogue. For their work on the Web site, we applaud Laura Kleger, Associate Director, Web Site; Jennifer Otten, Senior Interactive Web Designer; Gregory Gestner, Assistant Editor, Web Site; and Sean Redmond, Web Developer.

We offer our sincere appreciation to the Development Department for its efforts to secure support for this exhibition: John L. Wielk, Executive Director of Corporate and Institutional Development; Brynn Myers, Director of Institutional Development; Helen Warwick, Executive Director of Individual Development; Bronwyn Keenan, Director of Special Events; Ben Whine, Associate Director of Individual Development; and Rachel Nawi, Manager of Institutional Development. In External Affairs, we are grateful for the efforts of Eleanor R. Goldhar, Deputy Director and Chief of Global Communications, Solomon R. Guggenheim Foundation; Betsy Ennis, Director of Media and Public Relations; Laura Miller, Director of Marketing; Lauren Van Natten, Senior Publicist; and Claire Laporte, Publicist. We thank Maria Celi, Director of Visitor Services and Retail Operations; Ed Fuqua, Merchandise Manager; and Katherine Lock, Merchandise Manager. The Education Department is instrumental in ensuring that this exhibition reaches its audience, and we extend our gratitude to Kim Kanatani, Deputy Director and Gail Engelberg Director of Education, Solomon R. Guggenheim Foundation; Christina Yang, Associate Director of Education, Public Programs; Sharon Vatsky, Associate Director of Education, School and Family Programs; and Rachel Sirota, Manager of Public Programs.

Furthermore, this exhibition would not have been possible without the indispensable assistance of many individuals outside the museum who kindly responded to our various research inquiries and requests, including Jacqueline Matisse Monnier and Paul B. Franklin, Association Marcel Duchamp, Villiers-sous-Grez, France; Barbara Buckley, Judith Dolkart, and Margaret Little, Barnes Foundation, Merion, Pennsylvania; Isabelle Jansen, Gabriele Münter- und Johannes Eichner-Stiftung, Munich; Kendra Roth, Metropolitan Museum of Art, New York; Lynda Zycherman, Museum of Modern Art, New York; Sally Malenka and Melissa Meighan, Philadelphia Museum of Art; Annegret Hoberg and Susanne Boeller, Städtische Galerie im Lenbachhaus, Munich; and Günter Herzog, Zentralarchiv des internationalen Kunsthandels (ZADIK), Cologne. We are especially grateful to the anonymous individual who augmented the presentation by graciously lending works from a private collection, and, in doing so, helped us to more fully tell our story.

And finally, we are deeply indebted to the Peggy Guggenheim Collection and its director Philip Rylands, as well as to the Gianni Mattioli Collection and Laura Mattioli for their support of and commitment to this project. It is a delight to see so many treasures of modern art from New York and Venice assembled together under one roof, and we appreciate this opportunity to showcase the foundation's illustrious collection.

TRACEY BASHKOFF
Curator of Collections and Exhibitions
Solomon R. Guggenheim Museum

MEGAN M. FONTANELLA
Assistant Curator of Collections and Provenance
Solomon R. Guggenheim Museum

INTRODUCTION

TRACEY BASHKOFF AND MEGAN M. FONTANELLA

The great upheaval,
The shifting emphasis in art, literature, and music,
The multifariousness of form, the constructive principle, the composition
of these forms,
The intensive turn to the inner realm of nature and, associated with it,
the rejection of the beautification of nature's exterior—
—Such are, generally sketched out, the signs of the new inner renaissance.

ANNOUNCEMENT OF THE FIRST DER BLAUE REITER EXHIBITION, 1911[1]

When Vasily Kandinsky and Franz Marc formed the group Der Blaue Reiter (The Blue Rider) in late 1911, the artists predicted a watershed in the arts, a *große Umwälzung* (great upheaval) that would radically challenge traditional modes of artistic production (fig. 1). Undoubtedly, tremendous creativity and innovation characterized the years leading up to World War I, especially 1910 to 1914. European cities were evolving, and the artistic avant-garde likewise adapted and responded to twentieth-century modernity, from its spectacles and technological feats to the social fragmentation and alienation of the modern metropolis. Ever more artists banded together in groups, a phenomenon that not only increased an artist's chance of public exposure through collective exhibitions, but also encouraged greater experimentation and facilitated means of interchange. The extraordinary output of manifestos, treatises, and theoretical writings—another hallmark of the period—contributed to the dissemination of radically new art forms across artistic and geographic boundaries. Alluding to the infamous marketing strategies of the Italian Futurists in particular, art critic Roger Allard noted: "With the aid of articles in the press, shrewdly organized exhibitions, contradictory lectures, polemics, manifestos, proclamations, prospectuses, and other futurist publicity, a painter or a group of painters is launched."[2] *The Great Upheaval: Modern Art from the Guggenheim Collection, 1910–1918* not only illuminates the dynamism of this fertile period, as artists hurtled toward abstraction and the ultimate "great upheaval" of a catastrophic war, but also highlights the masterpieces of modern art that launched the museum's collection.

THE SPIRIT OF THE TIME

As poet and art critic Guillaume Apollinaire boldly proclaimed in 1912, "the Cubists, no matter to which faction they belong, appear to all of us who are concerned with the future of art to be the most serious and interesting artists of our time."[3] Inspired by Paul Cézanne's geometrized compositions, Georges Braque and Pablo Picasso originated Cubism in France around 1908, simplifying and fracturing objects into faceted forms and emphasizing the flat plane of the canvas. The technique blossomed with stunning rapidity and led others to experiment with fragmentation and simultaneity (depicting multiple views) or the movement of bodies and objects through space. Unlike their Expressionist colleagues in Austria and Germany, who sought to convey spirituality in art and promoted freedom from what they deemed a materialist bourgeois society, formalist concerns remained paramount to the Cubists.

Braque and Picasso were essential to the Parisian avant-garde, but the two rarely participated in salons or other group shows. The artists known as "Les Cubistes" were instead those

Fig. 1 Large-format brochure announcing *Die erste Ausstellung der Redaktion Der Blaue Reiter* (*First Exhibition of the Blaue Reiter Editorial Office*, Moderne Galerie Heinrich Thannhauser, Munich, December 18, 1911–January 3, 1912), second of three pages

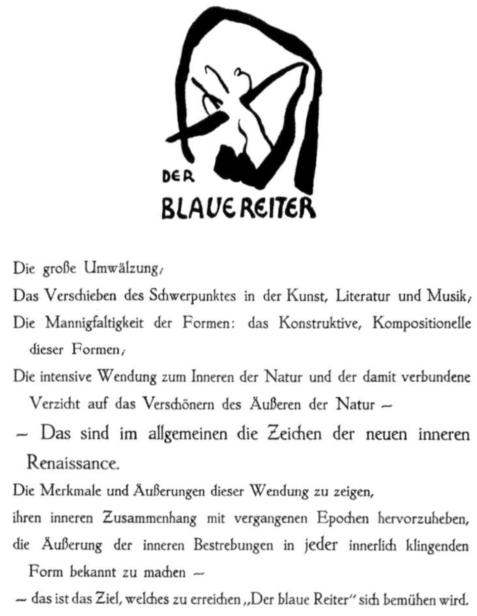

DER
BLAUE REITER

Die große Umwälzung,
Das Verschieben des Schwerpunktes in der Kunst, Literatur und Musik,
Die Mannigfaltigkeit der Formen: das Konstruktive, Kompositionelle dieser Formen,
Die intensive Wendung zum Inneren der Natur und der damit verbundene Verzicht auf das Verschönern des Äußeren der Natur –
– Das sind im allgemeinen die Zeichen der neuen inneren Renaissance.
Die Merkmale und Äußerungen dieser Wendung zu zeigen,
ihren inneren Zusammenhang mit vergangenen Epochen hervorzuheben,
die Äußerung der inneren Bestrebungen in jeder innerlich klingenden Form bekannt zu machen –
– das ist das Ziel, welches zu erreichen „Der blaue Reiter" sich bemühen wird.

Fig. 2 Salon d'Automne, Paris, October 1–November 8, 1912. Large-scale paintings by František Kupka, Jean Metzinger, and Francis Picabia are on view; in the foreground are sculptures by Amedeo Modigliani alongside small Cubist pictures

who collectively exhibited their work in public venues: Alexander Archipenko, the Duchamp brothers (Marcel Duchamp, Raymond Duchamp-Villon, and Jacques Villon), Henri Le Fauconnier, Albert Gleizes, Juan Gris, František Kupka, Fernand Léger, and Jean Metzinger, among others.[4] These artists gathered at Villon's Puteaux studio, Gleizes's Courbevoie studio, and the lively cafés of Paris. As Gleizes later explained, "It seemed essential to us then that we should form a group, see more of each other, and exchange ideas."[5] Despite the intense derision and public criticism unleashed against the Cubists in their first collective showing in Salle 41 of the 1911 Salon des Indépendants, the movement nonetheless gained full recognition in Paris by 1912. That year, the Cubists were featured in three major exhibitions: the Salon des Indépendants, the Salon d'Automne (fig. 2), and most importantly, the artist-organized Salon de la Section d'Or.[6]

The Italian Futurists, whose stylistic idiom incorporated Cubist and Divisionist techniques, were perhaps the most cohesive group to emerge during the prewar period. The movement's first manifesto, written by Filippo Tommaso Marinetti, was published in February 1909 in the Paris newspaper *Le Figaro*, and the next year a second manifesto signed by Giacomo Balla, Umberto Boccioni, Carlo Carrà, Luigi Russolo, and Gino Severini laid the foundation for Futurism's painterly expression. Futurist manifestos of sculpture, music, noise, photography, theater, architecture, cinema, and politics followed.[7] As with many artists inhabiting the burgeoning European art centers in the 1910s, the exuberance and speed of modern life was a source of constant inspiration to the Futurists, who additionally glorified the dynamism and violence of the new technological society. A major traveling exhibition in 1912, and the notoriously well-organized publicity campaign that accompanied it, solidified the Futurists' place as major players on the international stage.

Members of the Russian avant-garde, including Natalia Goncharova, Mikhail Larionov, and Kazimir Malevich, briefly experimented with combining the fractured spaces of Cubism with the Futurist synchronicity of shifting forms. Traditional sources such as folk art and icon painting informed their work as well. The first Bubnovyi valet (Jack of Diamonds) exhibition of 1910 marked a significant gathering of Russians with their Western colleagues, but the following year, Goncharova and Larionov founded in opposition the association Oslinyi khvost (Donkey's Tail). Their first exhibition in 1912 recognized the singular innovations of the Russian avant-garde.[8] Around this time Larionov also developed Rayism, which incorporated elements of the Impressionist representation of light, Cubist fragmentation, and Futurist lines of force, while Malevich pioneered Suprematism, an abstract style that aimed to express universal truths through the interrelationship of color and geometric form.

Many more modernist groups proliferated in the prewar period, each asserting the primacy of its own style and fighting for public recognition. But despite differing social, political, and aesthetic preoccupations, a growing trend toward internationalism and synthesis emerged in the arts. As the Blaue Reiter stated in the brochure for its premier exhibition in 1911, "we do not wish to propagate a *single* precise and special form, rather we intend to demonstrate through the *diversity* of the represented forms how the *inner desire* of the artists manifests itself multifariously."[9] Other heterogeneous and transnational exhibitions followed. In March 1912 alone, major exhibitions in Moscow, Munich, and Paris shared common participants, thus testifying to the cross-pollination of the international avant-garde. French artists Maurice de Vlaminck and Robert Delaunay exhibited in both the Salon des Indépendants in Paris and the second Blaue

Fig. 3 Announcement for the Erster deutscher Herbstsalon (First German Autumn Salon, Der Sturm, Berlin, September 20–December 1, 1913)

ERSTER DEUTSCHER HERBSTSALON
DER STURM
75 POTSDAMER STRASSE 75 • ECKE PALLASSTR.

Expressionisten — Kubisten — Futuristen

Deutschland — Amerika — Böhmen
Frankreich — Holland — Indien — Italien
Oesterreich — Rumänien — Russland
Schweiz — Spanien — Türkei

Täglich auch Sonntags 10—7 • Eintritt 1 Mark
Vom 20. September bis 1. Dezember

DER STURM

Ständige Kunstausstellung :: Monatlicher Wechsel
:: Halbmonatsschrift mit Originalgraphik ::
Verein für Kunst :: Vorlesungen und Vorträge

Ausstellungsräume und Verwaltung:
Potsdamer Strasse 134a am Potsdamer Platz

DER STURM • DIREKTION HERWARTH WALDEN

Reiter exhibition in Munich; Russian émigré Marc Chagall in the Salon des Indépendants and the Oslinyi khvost exhibition in Moscow; and Russians Goncharova and Malevich in the Oslinyi khvost and Blaue Reiter exhibitions.[10] The 1913 Erster deutscher Herbstsalon (First German Autumn Salon), at Herwarth Walden's Der Sturm gallery in Berlin, astonishingly featured some eighty-five artists from thirteen countries (fig. 3). More than 360 works were on view, including the original plaster cast of Boccioni's *Unique Forms of Continuity in Space* (*Forme uniche della continuità nello spazio*, 1913 [cast 2005], p. 149); Goncharova's *Cats (rayist percep.[tion] in rose, black, and yellow)* (*Koshki [luchistoe vospr.(iiatie) rozovoe, chernoe i zheltoe]*, 1913, p. 150); Kandinsky's *Painting with White Border* (*Bild mit weissem Rand*, May 1913, p. 155); and Léger's *Nude Model in the Studio* (*Le modèle nu dans l'atelier*, 1912–13, p. 119).

THE ART OF HIS TIME

The Guggenheim Museum's engagement with the modern period began nine years after the 1918 cease-fire, with a portentous meeting between founder Solomon R. Guggenheim and the young German artist Hilla Rebay. Rebay was commissioned to paint the retired industrialist's portrait in late 1927, but what transpired from this meeting was a fruitful collaboration that would last until Guggenheim's death. Under Rebay's guidance, the focus of the art collection Guggenheim had formed with his wife, Irene Rothschild, shifted dramatically away from the old master paintings, French Barbizon school, American landscapes, and other similar work that was fashionable within their circle. Instead, in 1929 Guggenheim began enthusiastically collecting the art of his time and especially exponents of nonobjectivity, an art form that aspired to spiritual or utopian aims. He simultaneously began to amass prime examples of European modernism.[11]

Besides facilitating visits to artist studios, Rebay encouraged Guggenheim to collect certain artists' work in-depth and from various points in their oeuvres. During their 1930 tour of Europe, Rebay personally introduced the Guggenheims to Chagall, Robert and Sonia Delaunay, Gleizes, Léger, and Piet Mondrian in Paris. Guggenheim would ultimately acquire more than one picture by all of these artists. From Chagall's prewar period, the Guggenheims had already acquired *Paris Through the Window* (*Paris par la fenêtre*, 1913, p. 141), a painting that Rebay located for them in Berlin in 1929 (but wished to have purchased for herself).[12] Robert Delaunay's *Eiffel Tower* (*Tour Eiffel*, 1911, p. 78) was purchased directly from the artist in 1930, and *Eiffel Tower with Trees* (*Tour Eiffel aux arbres*, summer 1910, p. 53) and *Red Eiffel Tower* (*La tour rouge*, 1911–12, p. 79) were added to the collection in 1946, thus allowing the museum to represent this artist, and one of his career-defining series, more fully to this day. In the summer of 1930, the Guggenheims met Rudolf Bauer at his Berlin studio and Kandinsky at the Dessau Bauhaus. Both would become core artists of the founding collection. Bauer, who was involved in a complicated personal relationship with Rebay, would also act as Guggenheim's European agent and advisor through the next decade and help secure many pivotal works for his collection.

The Solomon R. Guggenheim Foundation was established in June 1937 with the Guggenheims' collection, which in the following two years doubled in size from approximately four hundred works to nearly eight hundred.[13] In 1939 the foundation opened the Museum of Non-Objective Painting (forerunner to the Solomon R. Guggenheim Museum) with Rebay serving as its director and curator. Bauer's and Kandinsky's nonobjective work

Fig. 4 Solomon and Irene Guggenheim's suite at the Plaza Hotel, New York, with works on view including Marc Chagall's *Paris Through the Window* (*Paris par la fenêtre*, 1913, p. 141) at right, ca. 1931

Fig. 5 Gianni Mattioli's flat in Via Senato 36, Milan, where his collection was open to the public from 1950 to 1967; works by Giacomo Balla, Umberto Boccioni, Luigi Russolo, and Gino Severini are on view

predominated, however the Guggenheims continued to acquire and hang in their personal residence what Rebay termed "paintings with an object"[14] (fig. 4). Rebay likewise recognized that chronological and stylistic gaps in the collection remained. She wrote to Bauer in 1938: "Where can one get a Futurist picture? A Severini or a Balla? This is missing from our collection."[15] Severini's *Red Cross Train Passing a Village* (*Train de la Croix Rouge traversant un village*, summer 1915, p. 181) entered the collection in 1944. Moreover, the estate of émigré dealer Karl Nierendorf was acquired in 1948 and included a significant number of Expressionist works by Kandinsky, Paul Klee, and Marc, as well as such masterpieces as Oskar Kokoschka's *Knight Errant* (*Der irrende Ritter*, 1915, p. 185).[16] The following year Rebay purchased Marc's *Yellow Cow* (*Gelbe Kuh*, 1911, p. 75) from Nell Urech-Walden, the second wife of the avant-garde dealer Walden. Along with Delaunay's *The City* (*La ville*, 1911, p. 77), *Yellow Cow* was shown in the 1911 Blaue Reiter exhibition. Rebay also secured from Urech-Walden Chagall's *The Soldier Drinks* (*Le soldat boit*, 1911–12, p. 87) and *The Flying Carriage* (*La calèche volante*, 1913, p. 140), both of which she had seen hanging at Der Sturm more than thirty years prior.[17]

Following Guggenheim's death in 1949 and the end of Rebay's tenure as director shortly thereafter, subsequent directors afforded the modern collection a prominent place in the exhibition galleries of the museum's Frank Lloyd Wright–designed building, which opened in 1959. The collection also continued to grow. Major paintings by members of the Russian avant-garde, including Goncharova's *Cats (rayist percep.[tion] in rose, black, and yellow)* and Larionov's *Glass* (*Steklo*, 1912, p. 108), were purchased from each artist in the 1950s under director James Johnson Sweeney. Also in this decade, the foundation's sculpture collection expanded significantly with the acquisition of pieces by Archipenko, Constantin Brancusi, Duchamp-Villon, Jacques Lipchitz, and Amedeo Modigliani. The collection did not include a Henri Matisse painting until as late as 1982 (*The Italian Woman* [*L'Italienne*], 1916, p. 194), whereas a small group of paintings by Picasso, including his elusive Cubist portrait *Accordionist* (*L'Accordéoniste*, summer

1911, p. 81), had been acquired in 1936.[18] Some thirty additional Picassos, spanning sixty-five years of his career, entered the collection in 1978 and 1991 with Justin K. and Hilde Thannhauser's major donations of nineteenth- and early-twentieth-century art.[19] The Thannhauser Collection, acquired under director Thomas M. Messer, extended the scope of the foundation's holdings to include the precursors of modern art, such as Cézanne, Paul Gauguin, and Vincent van Gogh, whose work greatly influenced the next generation of avant-garde painters.

Another especially noteworthy acquisition was Peggy Guggenheim's collection in Venice, and the palazzo that houses it, which she transferred to the foundation in 1976. Peggy's motto "buy a picture a day" led her to amass phenomenal holdings that reveal her predilection for the art of the Surrealists and the early New York school.[20] Many of her acquisitions were the result of her patronage of artists—not unlike Rebay and Solomon R. Guggenheim. Moreover, the fact that Peggy's collecting habits vastly differed from those of her uncle was fortuitous for the foundation. Highlights from the modern period include Duchamp's *Nude (Study), Sad Young Man on a Train* (*Nu [esquisse], jeune homme triste dans un train*, 1911–12, p. 91) and an untitled Suprematist painting by Malevich (ca. 1916, p. 193). Both artists were previously underrepresented in the Guggenheim collection in New York.[21]

Finally, *The Great Upheaval* includes a number of prime examples of Italian Futurism from the Gianni Mattioli Collection, which has been on long-term loan to the Peggy Guggenheim Collection since 1997. Gianni Mattioli spent his childhood in Milan in an apartment just a few yards from the residence of Marinetti, the leader of the Futurist movement.[22] In the interwar years, Mattioli formed a close friendship with the artist Fortunato Depero, and he associated with Balla, Russolo, Severini, and Marinetti himself, among others. He ultimately established 1909—the year Marinetti published the first Futurist manifesto—as the definitive starting point for his art collection, the bulk of which was acquired in the late 1940s and early 1950s (fig. 5). Boccioni especially came to be represented in depth and with such masterpieces as *Materia* (1912) and *Dynamism of a Cyclist* (*Dinamismo di un ciclista*, 1913, p. 147), in addition to the definitive study for his radical painting *The City Rises* (1910), (Study for *The City Rises* [Studio per *La città che sale*], 1910, p. 55). Looking back on his years as a collector, Mattioli wrote in 1967: "As a modest water-diviner, I have tried to locate and to signal the underground streams from which come the waters of the tumultuous river of the painting and sculpture, which, in the years immediately before the Great War, have changed the face and the present-day concept of art."[23]

Today the museum's holdings of modern art are by no means complete. Nonetheless, they reflect the visions of the individuals who shaped the collection, beginning with Solomon R. Guggenheim and Hilla Rebay, and their personal tastes and relationships with particular artists, collectors, and dealers alike. *The Great Upheaval* unites the Guggenheim Foundation's remarkable collections in New York and Venice in order to trace the origins of the museum and capture the spirit and dynamism of the European avant-garde in the 1910s. Moreover, the essays that follow investigate a defining aspect of each year leading up to and including the war years, from the visual and literary attributes of the time, to the people and events that changed the course of modernism.

Notes

1 Excerpt from a large-format brochure announcing *Die erste Ausstellung der Redaktion Der Blaue Reiter*, 1911, p. 2 (see fig. 1), quoted in Reinhold Heller, "The Blue Rider," *Schoenberg, Kandinsky, and the Blue Rider*, exh. cat. (New York: Jewish Museum and Scala Publishers, 2003), p. 74. While the brochure does not list an author, the original manuscript is in Vasily Kandinsky's hand. See Vasily Kandinsky and Franz Marc, eds., *The Blaue Reiter Almanac*, new documentary edition, ed. Klaus Lankheit, trans. Henning Falkenstein (Boston: MFA Publications, 2008), pp. 246–47.

2 Roger Allard, "Les arts plastiques—Le Salon d'automne," *Les ecrits français*, December 5, 1914, p. 64, quoted in Jeffrey Weiss, *The Popular Culture of Modern Art: Picasso, Duchamp, and Avant-Gardism* (New Haven, Conn.: Yale University Press, 1994), p. 60.

3 Guillaume Apollinaire, *La Section d'Or*, October 9, 1912, quoted in Lisa Dennison, "1912," *The Guggenheim Collection*, exh. cat. (New York: Guggenheim Museum, 2006), p. 95.

4 Ibid., p. 96.

5 Albert Gleizes, *Souvenirs, le cubisme, 1908–1914*, Cahiers Albert Gleizes, I (Lyon, France: L'association des amis d'Albert Gleizes, 1957), quoted in Milton A. Cohen, *Movement, Manifesto, Melee: The Modernist Group, 1910–1914* (Lanham, Md.: Lexington Books, 2004), p. 5.

6 The Salon de la Section d'Or was solely devoted to Cubism and reached a broad international audience as it traveled to London, Berlin, Amsterdam, Vienna, Dresden, and Moscow. See Bruce Altshuler, ed., *Salon to Biennial—Exhibitions That Made Art History, Volume 1: 1863–1959* (London: Phaidon Press Limited, 2008), pp. 129–38, and entries on "The First Blaue Reiter Exhibition, Munich, 1911," pp. 99–110; "Les Peintures Futuristes Italiens, Paris, 1912," pp. 111–26; and "The First German Autumn Salon, Berlin, 1913," pp. 139–50.

7 See Lawrence Rainey, Christine Poggi, and Laura Wittman, eds., *Futurism: An Anthology* (New Haven, Conn.: Yale University Press, 2009).

8 Natalia Goncharova and Mikhail Larionov objected to the prominence and attention given to French art in the Bubnovyi valet exhibitions of 1910 and 1912. The 1912 Oslinyi khvost exhibition consisted of some three hundred works by Goncharova, Larionov, Kazimir Malevich, Vladimir Tatlin, and minor members of the Moscow avant-garde. It is interesting that the exhibition also included Marc Chagall, who resided in Paris and was decidedly influenced by his French and German colleagues.

9 *Die erste Ausstellung der Redaktion Der Blaue Reiter*, 1911, quoted in Heller, "The Blue Rider," p. 74 (Kandinsky's and Marc's emphasis).

10 Dennison, "1912," pp. 132, 136.

11 See *Solomon R. Guggenheim Collection of Non-Objective Paintings*, exh. cat. (Charleston, S.C.: Gibbes Memorial Art Gallery, 1936), p. 41. Organized by Carolina Art Association.

12 For in-depth discussions of the genesis of the Guggenheim Foundation, see Joan M. Lukach, *Hilla Rebay: In Search of the Spirit in Art* (New York: George Braziller, 1983), and Karole Vail, ed., *The Museum of Non-Objective Painting: Hilla Rebay and the Origins of the Solomon R. Guggenheim Museum* (New York: Guggenheim Museum, 2009).

13 Hilla Rebay to Rudolf Bauer, November 11, 1929, Hilla von Rebay Foundation Archives (hereafter cited as HVRF Archives), M0007, Solomon R. Guggenheim Museum Archives (hereafter cited as SRGM Archives), cited in Lukach, *Hilla Rebay*, pp. 71–72.

14 Lukach, *Hilla Rebay*, p. 106.

15 Hilla Rebay to Rudolf Bauer, 1938, HVRF Archives, M0007, SRGM Archives, quoted in ibid., p. 105.

16 For more on Karl Nierendorf and the museum's 1948 purchase of his estate, see Megan M. Fontanella, "'Unity in Diversity': Karl Nierendorf and America, 1937–47," *American Art* 24, no. 3 (Fall 2010), pp. 114–25.

17 Lukach, *Hilla Rebay*, p. 72.

18 Solomon R. Guggenheim and Hilla Rebay had preferred to buy directly from artists whenever possible, but in the 1930s it was difficult to obtain works by such artists as Henri Matisse and Pablo Picasso without going through their dealers. See ibid., p. 95.

19 Justin K. Thannhauser was the son of Heinrich Thannhauser, founder of the Moderne Galerie in Munich. For more information on the Thannhauser Collection, see Vivian Endicott Barnett, *The Guggenheim Museum: Justin K. Thannhauser Collection* (New York: Solomon R. Guggenheim Foundation, 1978), and Matthew Drutt, ed., *Thannhauser: The Thannhauser Collection of the Guggenheim Museum* (New York: Guggenheim Museum, 2001).

20 Peggy Guggenheim, *Out of This Century: Confessions of an Art Addict* (New York: Universe Books, 1979), p. 209.

21 For more on the subject of Peggy Guggenheim, see Susan Davidson and Philip Rylands, eds., *Peggy Guggenheim & Frederick Kiesler: The Story of Art of This Century* (New York: Guggenheim Museum, 2004).

22 The biography of Gianni Mattioli is drawn from Laura Mattioli Rossi, "Gianni Mattioli," *Masterpieces from the Gianni Mattioli Collection* (Venice: Peggy Guggenheim Collection, 1997), pp. 9–20.

23 Typewritten notes by Gianni Mattioli; November 1967, Mattioli Archive, Milan, quoted in ibid., p. 19.

1910

JANUARY Bernheim-Jeune gallery, Paris, presents a **Paul Cézanne** exhibition. • First Futurist evening takes place at the Politeama Rossetti theater in Trieste, Italy. • Early in the year, *Zolotoe runo* (1906–10) releases in Moscow its last two journal issues, which were created in 1909.

FEBRUARY A major **Henri Matisse** exhibition occurs at Bernheim-Jeune. • Aroldo Bonzagni, **Umberto Boccioni**, **Carlo Carrà**, Romolo Romani, **Luigi Russolo**, and **Gino Severini** sign the "Manifesto dei pittori futuristi" ("Manifesto of Futurist Painters") in Milan. • Franz Josef Brakl's Moderne Kunsthandlung organizes Franz Marc's first solo exhibition.

MARCH Soiuz molodezhi (Union of Youth) group is founded in Saint Petersburg and has its first exhibition concurrent with the premier show of Nikolai Kulbin's Treugolnik (Triangle) group. • *Pan* (1895–1900; 1910–15), a journal edited by dealer Paul Cassirer and art historian Wilhelm Herzog, resumes publication, and *Der Sturm* (1910–32), edited by gallerist Herwarth Walden and devoted to avant-garde literature, art, and music, begins publication in Berlin.

APRIL Halley's Comet appears. • **Giacomo Balla**, **Boccioni**, **Carrà**, **Russolo**, and **Severini** sign the "Manifesto tecnico della pittura futurista" ("Technical Manifesto of Futurist Painting") in Milan. • In early spring, Filippo Tommaso Marinetti gives several lectures in London where he reads the "Fondazione e manifesto del futurismo" ("Founding and Manifesto of Futurism," 1909).

MAY George V succeeds Edward VII as King of England on May 6 and is crowned in 1911. • Max Pechstein founds with Georg Tappert the Neue Secession after the Berliner Secession rejects works by a number of members of Die Brücke (The Bridge), a group formed in 1905 by Erich Heckel, **Ernst Ludwig Kirchner**, and Karl Schmidt-Rottluff (Pechstein joined in 1906 and Otto Müller in 1910).

JUNE First commercial passenger flight carries twelve passengers and eight crew members from Friedrichshafen, Germany, to Düsseldorf. • Igor Stravinsky's *L'oiseau de feu*

Names in bold refer to artists in the exhibition.

1910

(*The Firebird*, 1909–10), the first original score written expressly for Sergei Diaghilev's Ballets Russes, premieres in Paris. • Galerie Paul Cassirer, Berlin, presents **Oskar Kokoschka**'s first solo exhibition.

JULY Considered the first Expressionist play, **Kokoschka**'s *Mörder, Hoffnung der Frauen* (Murderer, hope of women) is published in *Der Sturm*.

AUGUST **Marc Chagall** arrives in Paris from his native Russia. • Kunstmuseum, Bern, presents **Paul Klee**'s first solo exhibition.

SEPTEMBER Under Pope Pius X, the Vatican mandates an oath against modernism. • **Henri Rousseau** dies. • Moderne Galerie Heinrich Thannhauser organizes the second exhibition of the Neue Künstlervereinigung München (NKVM) (New Artists' Association of Munich), a group formed by **Alexei Jawlensky**, **Vasily Kandinsky**, Gabriele Münter, and Marianne von Werefkin in 1909. • Galerie Ernst Arnold, Dresden, mounts a Brücke exhibition.

OCTOBER First infrared photographs are published in the journal of the Royal Photographic Society in London.

NOVEMBER Roger Fry coins the term "Post-Impressionism" on the occasion of the exhibition *Manet and the Post-Impressionists*, which he organizes for the Grafton Galleries in London.

DECEMBER **Mikhail Larionov** founds the Bubnovyi valet (Jack of Diamonds) group in Moscow. Its nucleus consists of **Natalia Goncharova, Larionov**, and several students expelled from the Moscow Institute of Painting, Sculpture, and Architecture. The group's first exhibition, at the Salon of the Levisson Building, Moscow, also includes work by **Kandinsky**, **Kazimir Malevich**, and Russian Futurists David and Vladimir Burliuk. • Premier Moscow Salon features work by **Goncharova**, **Larionov**, and **Malevich**. • Dutch painter and critic Conrad Kickert founds the Moderne Kunstkring (Modern Art Circle) in Amsterdam. • By the end of the year, **Pablo Picasso** has garnered support from art dealers Daniel-Henry Kahnweiler, Wilhelm Uhde, and Ambroise Vollard.

Pages 24–25: From left: Marcel Duchamp, Jacques Villon, Raymond Duchamp-Villon, and Villon's dog Pipe in the garden of Villon's studio, Puteaux, France, ca. 1913

"OF THIS CENTURY": PAST GENERATIONS AND NEW BEGINNINGS

TRACEY BASHKOFF

You will no longer find that amazing in the future. And I have been told before that I was not of this century.

HENRI ROUSSEAU, 1910[1]

When defending one of his final paintings, Henri Rousseau wrote that the fascination with its imagery, or with his unwavering style and determination to maintain it, would not last. He appears aware that his work would give way to the artistic innovations of the time. Shown in the 1910 Salon des Indépendants, Rousseau's *The Dream* (*Le rêve*, 1910) featured, in his characteristic, flattened, naïve manner, the incongruous image of a recumbent nude woman on a deep red sofa situated in a lush jungle. Rousseau responded to the salon's perplexed viewers: "You shouldn't be surprised to find a sofa out in a virgin forest. It means nothing except for the richness of the red. You understand, the sofa is in a room; the rest is Yadwigha's dream."[2] Rousseau had a remarkable talent for taking an outmoded, folk art–inspired painting style and making it relevant to the next generation of artists, although he was not widely recognized for this achievement during his lifetime (fig. 6). Stylistically simple, his work's sophistication was understated and appealed to the avant-garde. A fixture in Paris through the turn of the twentieth century, he was nicknamed "Le Douanier" (customs officer) because of his early occupation as a tax collector. Perhaps because the subjects of his canvases were more exotic than his own travels, the moniker endured. Moreover, the emerging generation of avant-garde painters admired his work;[3] Pablo Picasso, for instance, owned five of his canvases at one point. Rousseau in turn respected the younger artist and astutely commented on the strengths they each brought to their oeuvres: "We are the two great painters of this era, you in Egyptian style, I in modern style."[4] He recognized the primitive in Picasso and the avant-garde in his own work. When Rousseau died on September 2, 1910, most Parisians were still on holiday, and only his family and artist Paul Signac attended his funeral. Rousseau's landlord and the artist Robert Delaunay paid for a thirty-year plot in a Paris cemetery and erected a headstone with a bronze medallion. Poet Guillaume Apollinaire wrote a verse for Rousseau's epitaph in chalk, and then in 1913, sculptor Constantin Brancusi engraved the words: "Let our baggage through free at heaven's gate/We shall bring your brushes and paints and canvas/So that you can devote your sacred leisure in the light of truth."[5]

Rousseau, along with Paul Cézanne, Paul Gauguin, Vincent van Gogh, and the Fauves, was among the painters who had the greatest impact on emerging artists in first decades of the twentieth century. The continuum of influence was nourished by direct contact, as in the case of Rousseau's presence in Paris or the publication of his first monograph, authored by dealer Wilhelm Uhde, in 1911.[6] Furthermore, as new groups coalesced and established their own exhibition opportunities in Paris,

Munich, Moscow, and other major European cities, significant showings of their immediate predecessors occurred. The prominent Bernheim-Jeune gallery in Paris presented a Cézanne retrospective in January 1910, which included *Still Life: Plate of Peaches* (*Assiette de pêches*, 1879–80, p. 35), followed by a smaller exhibition at Ambroise Vollard's gallery, *Figures de Cézanne* (*Cézanne's Figures*), which occasioned Apollinaire to remark: "Most of the new painters admit their debt to this sincere and candid artist."[7] In August 1910, the recently established Moderne Galerie Heinrich Thannhauser in Munich presented a major Gauguin exhibition with Ludwig Gutbier's Galerie Ernst Arnold, which provided the second venue in Dresden. The exhibition showcased, among other works, *Haere Mai* (1891, p. 37) from Vollard's collection. In Moscow, collector Sergei Shchukin began buying Post-Impressionist work in 1903–04, amassing examples by Cézanne, Gauguin, and Van Gogh, but by 1906 began energetically collecting works by Henri Matisse.[8] Young Russian artists such as Mikhail Larionov were reading translated texts by the more senior Nabis (Prophets) artists such as Maurice Denis as well as Matisse in 1909 and were above all influenced by their discussions of the use of "primitive" art forms. Most notably, two of the three *Zolotoe runo* (*Golden Fleece*) exhibitions held in Moscow between 1908 and 1910 prominently featured the previous twenty years of French modernism. Artists from Cézanne and Édouard Vuillard to the younger Albert Gleizes and Jean Metzinger were on view. In Italy the emerging Italian Futurists were looking to break from the past rather than emulate it.

Meanwhile in London, Roger Fry organized *Manet and the Post-Impressionists* at the Grafton Galleries from November 8, 1910, until January 15, 1911, essentially introducing the British

Fig. 6 Henri Rousseau in front of his painting *Forest Landscape with Setting Sun* (*Forêt vierge au soleil couchant*, ca. 1910), Paris, 1910

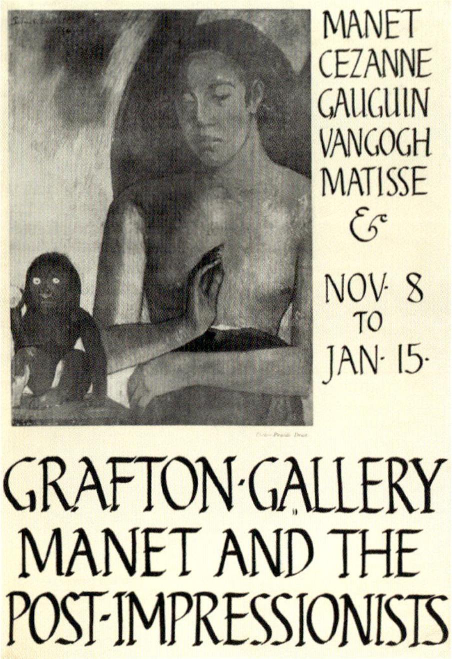

Fig. 7 Poster for the exhibition *Manet and the Post-Impressionists* (Grafton Galleries, London, November 8, 1910–January 15, 1911), 76.3 x 50.9 cm, featuring Paul Gauguin's *Poèmes barbares* (1896)

public to modernist painters who had long been seen in mainland Europe (fig. 7).[9] Fry hastily arranged the exhibition of more than two hundred paintings, sculptures, works on paper, and ceramics by drawing primarily on gallery and dealer holdings.[10] With this influential presentation, Fry canonized the term "Post-Impressionism" to cover work ranging from the 1880s through proto-Cubism, especially the art of Gauguin and Van Gogh. Also of significance, the exhibition placed current work by Picasso and other modernists in relation to their art-historical precursors. Despite the inclusion of such masterworks as Édouard Manet's *A Bar at the Folies-Bergère* (*Un bar aux Folies-Bergère*, 1882), Van Gogh's *Portrait of Dr. Gachet* (*Le docteur Paul Gachet*, 1890), and Gauguin's *Haere Mai*, the exhibition prompted vehement reaction from critics and visitors. One writer for London's *Morning Post* held the exhibition responsible "for revealing the existence of a wide-spread plot to destroy the whole fabric of European painting."[11] The controversial reactions even spread to the United States, where the story was picked up by the *New York Times* and other papers. Matthew Prichard, an administrator at the Museum of Fine Arts, Boston, and a friend of Fry, was one of the twenty-five thousand visitors to the exhibition. He wrote to collector Isabella Stewart Gardner: "Thanks to Fry, the post-impressionists—Cézanne, Gaugin [sic], Van Gogh and Matisse and the tail of the movement have reached London and have been received with shrieks of misunderstanding and interested horror."[12]

In Paris, at the 1910 Salon des Indépendants, celebrated by Apollinaire as "the rout of Impressionism," new works by Delaunay, Gleizes, Henri Le Fauconnier, Fernand Léger, and Metzinger were exhibited.[13] Critic Louis Vauxcelles called the artists "ignorant geometers, reducing the human body . . . to pallid cubes," but either way, the critics and the artists themselves recognized these shared stylistic concerns.[14] When the same artists, minus Léger, were hung in proximity to one another at the Salon d'Automne, writer Roger Allard referred to "analytical" forms and "synthesis" in describing their post Cézanne–inspired, planar compositions.[15]

Fig. 8 Umberto Boccioni, cartoon of the Futurist evening on March 18, 1910, at the Politeama Chiarella, Turin. On stage, from left: Carlo Carrà, Armando Mazza, Filippo Tommaso Marinetti, and Umberto Boccioni

Of seeing their work together, Gleizes recalled, "It was at this moment . . . that we discovered each other seriously . . . [and] realized what we had in common. The necessity of forming a group, of frequenting each other, of exchanging ideas seemed imperative."[16] In late 1910 they met at Le Fauconnier's studio to plan how they might influence the election of the hanging committee for the upcoming 1911 salon so that once again their work would be installed as a group.[17]

Many artists and writers who would come to be called Cubists—Gleizes, Roger de La Fresnaye, Léger, Metzinger, Robert and Sonia Delaunay, poet Jules Romains, among others—met with regularity at Le Fauconnier's studio, Closerie des Lilas café, and the salons of Gleizes and writer Alexandre Mercereau. The Parisian artists and writers discussed ideas and techniques as well as planned exhibitions, lectures, and opportunities for self-promotion. Brothers Marcel Duchamp, Raymond Duchamp-Villon, and Jacques Villon, along with their friend Francis Picabia formed the Société Normande de peinture moderne (Norman Society of Modern Painting), which later coalesced into the Puteaux group (pp. 24–25). The latter group gathered at Villon's studio in the Paris suburb on Sunday afternoons from around winter 1911 to 1914.[18] Gleizes later captured this effervescent moment: "1910 was the year when, in the last months, there joined together a kind of coherent group that represented certain precise tendencies for our generation, until then scattered. From the painters who met one another, joined by poets, sympathies were created, an ambiance was formed that was soon going to determine an action the effects of which would not be long in being felt outside [the circle]."[19] He added: "Painters and writers went forward shoulder to shoulder, animated by a sense of sharing the same faith."[20]

Also a movement of united literary and artistic aims, the Italian Futurist painters cohered in 1910, on their way to becoming the most influential and talked about group. Filippo Tommaso Marinetti's "Fondazione e manifesto del futurismo" ("Founding and Manifesto of Futurism") was published in the newspaper *Le Figaro* in February 1909. His audacious philosophy of life embraced youth, speed, violence, and technology while rejecting all ties to the past. The manifesto became an important promotional tool for the fledgling group, and two seminal painting manifestos published in the journal *Poesia* in 1910 heralded the birth of Futurism as an art movement. Marinetti was joined by painters Umberto Boccioni, Carlo Carrà, Luigi Russolo, and Gino Severini in signing, both in Milan, the "Manifesto dei pittori futuristi" ("Manifesto of Futurist Painters") in February and the "Manifesto tecnico della pittura futurista" ("Technical Manifesto of Futurist Painting") in April.[21] The former proclaimed: "Let the dead stay buried in the deepest entrails of the earth! Let the threshold of the future be swept free of mummies! Make room for the young, the violent, the bold!"[22] In January 1910 at the Politeama Rossetti theater in Trieste, Marinetti and Armando Mazza read the founding manifesto at the first Futurist evening. Additional evenings were held in cities across Italy, including Milan, Turin, and Venice. Beginning as readings of poetry and manifestos, the events nearly always turned sensational, devolving into insults and fistfights (fig. 8). Furthermore, in March 1910, the first exhibition of Futurist painting opened in Milan at the Famiglia Artistica.

The burgeoning Russian avant-garde developed around this time from smaller, loose associations in Moscow, Saint Petersburg, Odessa, and Kiev.[23] For instance, in March 1910, the Soiuz molodezhi (Union of Youth), founded in reaction to the more conservative Soiuz russkikh khudozhnikov (Union of Russian Artists), held its first exhibition in Saint Petersburg. The organization embraced a variety of stylistic approaches and was eager to involve progressive artists from other cities. Muskovites Natalia Goncharova, Larionov, and Ilya Mashkov were invited to exhibit with the group, marking the beginning of a fruitful collaboration between the avant-garde in Moscow and Saint Petersburg. Meanwhile in Odessa and Kiev, sculptor Vladimir Izdebsky's salon exhibited the work of the brothers David and Vladimir Burliuk, Goncharova, and Larionov as well as Russians living abroad, such as Alexei Jawlensky and Vasily Kandinsky. Larionov and Aristarkh Lentulov formed the Bubnovyi valet (Jack of Diamonds) in December as an exhibition society for young artists who objected to the policies of established groups. Larionov named the group either for the playing cards he and his colleagues collected from flea markets or from the mark put on political prisoners, a nod to the solidarity of social outcasts.[24] Staged at the Salon of the Levisson Building in Moscow that same month, the first Bubnovyi valet exhibition united thirty-eight artists affiliated with the Russian and European avant-garde, including Gleizes, Jawlensky, Kandinsky, Le Fauconnier, August Macke, Kazimir Malevich, Franz Marc, Metzinger, and Picasso.[25] The well-attended exhibition scandalized a public that was unaccustomed to the bright colors and rough forms. As one critic remarked, the work "infuriat[ed] the viewer's eye."[26] Lentulov also recalled, "Worthy people evaluated the exhibition with extreme disgust and indignation and attempted to leave quickly. . . . Critics and connoisseurs were bitterly quarreling. One could see here or there a group of people heatedly arguing, or surrounding an artist with clever questions and derisive remarks: 'Even I could have painted that,' 'This is a child's drawing,' 'This sketch is crudely done,' and so on, and so forth."[27]

The year 1910 marked a time of exciting new developments for the European avant-garde. The revolutionary painters of the previous generation—Cézanne, Rousseau, and the newly named Post-Impressionists, among others—continued to gain recognition and, as a result, exert a strong influence on younger modernists. As the public began to accept the old guard, artists from Paris to Milan to Moscow were increasingly experimenting with groundbreaking forms of visual expression and garnering public access through the growing number of salons and secession exhibitions. The year in many ways set the stage for the people and events that would come to define artistic production in the ensuing decade.

Notes

1 Henri Rousseau to "Monsieur" (French art critic), April 1, 1910, quoted in Roger Shattuck, *The Banquet Years: The Origins of the Avant-Garde in France, 1885 to World War I; Alfred Jarry, Henri Rousseau, Erik Satie, Guillaume Apollinaire* (New York: Vintage Books, 1968), p. 112.

2 Henri Rousseau to André Salmon, 1910, quoted in ibid., p. 111.

3 Vasily Kandinsky also owned at least two Henri Rousseau canvases; he included seven reproductions of Rousseau paintings in *Der Blaue Reiter* (*The Blaue Reiter Almanac*, 1912).

4 Ibid., p. 108.

5 Ibid., p. 76.

6 Wilhelm Uhde's publication includes a reproduction of *The Football Players* (*Les joueurs de football*, 1908, p. 41).

7 Adrianne O. Bratis, "Chronology," *Cézanne and Beyond*, exh. cat. (Philadelphia: Philadelphia Museum of Art; New Haven, Conn.: Yale University Press, 2009), p. 27.

8 Albert Kostenevich, "Sergei Shchukin: An Unsurpassed Collector with a Sense for the Unique and the Epoch-making," *Henri Matisse: Four Great Collectors*, ed. Kasper Monrad, exh. cat. (Copenhagen: Statens Museum for Kunst, 1999), pp. 75–79.

9 French gallerist Paul Durand-Ruel had sent an exhibition of three hundred Impressionist paintings to Grafton in 1905, but very little avant-garde work was subsequently shown. Bruce Altshuler, *Salon to Biennial: Exhibitions That Made Art History, Volume I: 1863–1959* (New York: Phaidon, 2008), p. 85.

10 Roger Fry also borrowed twelve works from Vincent van Gogh's sister-in-law. Ibid.

11 Robert Ross, "The Post-Impressionists at the Grafton: The Twilight of the Idols," *Morning Post*, London, November 7, 1910, quoted in ibid., p. 93.

12 Matthew Prichard to Isabella Stewart Gardner, November 22, 1910. Isabella Stewart Gardner Papers, Isabella Stewart Gardner Museum, quoted in Carol A. Nathanson, "The American Reaction to London's First Grafton Show," *Archives of American Art Journal* 25, no. 3 (1985), p. 3. As Nathanson points out, the 1910 Grafton show had an impact on American audiences, as well as European, in this period just prior to the 1913 *International Exhibition of Modern Art* (popularly known as the Armory Show) in New York, when the public's taste for French modernism was formed.

13 Milton A. Cohen, *Movement, Manifesto, Melee: The Modernist Group, 1910–1914* (Lanham, Md.: Lexington Books, 2004), p. 184.

14 Ibid.

15 Ibid., p. 185.

16 Albert Gleizes, *Souvenirs, le cubisme 1908–1914*, Cahiers Albert Gleizes, I (Lyon, France: L'association des amis d'Albert Gleizes, 1957), quoted in Cohen, *Movement, Manifesto, Melee*, p. 39.

17 Ibid., p. 185.

18 For a full listing of participants in artists' gatherings in Paris (as well as other cities), see Appendix 2, "Modernist Groups 1910–1914: A Listing," in Cohen, *Movement, Manifesto, Melee*, pp. 251–97.

19 Gleizes, *Souvenirs*, quoted in Cohen, *Movement, Manifesto, Melee*, p. 8.

20 Gleizes, *Souvenirs*, quoted in ibid., p. 60.

21 The first painting manifesto was also signed by Aroldo Bonzagni and Romolo Romani. The second manifesto was also signed by Giacomo Balla.

22 "Manifesto tecnico della pittura futurista" ("Technical Manifesto of Futurist Painting"), April 11, 1910, quoted in *Futurism: An Anthology*, ed. Lawrence Rainey, Christine Poggi, and Laura Wittman (New Haven, Conn.: Yale University Press, 2009), p. 64.

23 Camilla Gray, *The Great Experiment: Russian Art, 1863–1922* (New York: Abrams, 1962), p. 98.

24 Jane A. Sharp, "The Russian Avant-Garde and Its Audience: Moscow, 1913," *Modernism/Modernity* 6, no. 3 (September 1999), pp. 98–99, doi: 10.1353/mod.1999.0035.

25 John E. Bowlt, "Jacks and Tails," *Journal of the Walters Art Museum* 60/61 (2002/03), p. 15.

26 M. Voloshin, "Bubnovyi valet," *Russkaia khudozhestvennaia letopis'*, no. 1 (1911), p. 10, quoted in Bowlt, "Jacks and Tails," p. 16.

27 Aristarkh Lentulov, *Sieben Moskauer Künstler* (1984), p. 74, quoted in Anthony Parton, *Mikhail Larionov and the Russian Avant-Garde* (Princeton: Princeton University Press, 1993), p. 37.

PAUL CÉZANNE *Still Life: Plate of Peaches* (*Assiette de pêches*), 1879–80

Oil on canvas, 59.7 x 73.3 cm. Solomon R. Guggenheim Museum, New York

Thannhauser Collection, Gift, Justin K. Thannhauser 78.2514.4

VINCENT VAN GOGH *Mountains at Saint-Rémy* (*Montagnes à Saint-Rémy*), July 1889

Oil on canvas, 71.8 x 90.8 cm. Solomon R. Guggenheim Museum, New York

Thannhauser Collection, Gift, Justin K. Thannhauser 78.2514.24

PAUL GAUGUIN *Haere Mai*, 1891

Oil on burlap, 72.4 x 91.4 cm. Solomon R. Guggenheim Museum, New York

Thannhauser Collection, Gift, Justin K. Thannhauser 78.2514.16

PABLO PICASSO *Woman Ironing* (*La repasseuse*), Paris, spring 1904

Oil on canvas, 116.2 x 73 cm. Solomon R. Guggenheim Museum, New York

Thannhauser Collection, Gift, Justin K. Thannhauser 78.2514.41

HENRI ROUSSEAU *The Football Players* (*Les joueurs de football*), 1908

Oil on canvas, 100.3 x 80.3 cm. Solomon R. Guggenheim Museum, New York 60.1583

VASILY KANDINSKY *Blue Mountain* (*Der blaue Berg*), 1908–09

Oil on canvas, 106 x 96.6 cm. Solomon R. Guggenheim Museum, New York

Solomon R. Guggenheim Founding Collection, By gift 41.505

VASILY KANDINSKY Sketch for *Composition II* (Skizze für *Komposition II*), 1909–10

Oil on canvas, 97.5 x 131.2 cm. Solomon R. Guggenheim Museum, New York

Solomon R. Guggenheim Founding Collection 45.961

PABLO PICASSO *Carafe, Jug, and Fruit Bowl* (*Carafon, pot et compotier*), Horta de Ebro, summer 1909

Oil on canvas, 71.8 x 64.6 cm. Solomon R. Guggenheim Museum, New York

Solomon R. Guggenheim Founding Collection, By gift 37.536

ROBERT DELAUNAY *Saint-Séverin No. 3*, 1909–10

Oil on canvas, 114.1 x 88.6 cm. Solomon R. Guggenheim Museum, New York

Solomon R. Guggenheim Founding Collection, By gift 41.462

GEORGES BRAQUE *Violin and Palette* (*Violon et palette*), September 1, 1909
Oil on canvas, 91.7 x 42.8 cm. Solomon R. Guggenheim Museum, New York 54.1412

GEORGES BRAQUE *Piano and Mandola* (*Piano et mandore*), winter 1909–10

Oil on canvas, 91.7 x 42.8 cm. Solomon R. Guggenheim Museum, New York 54.1411

ERNST LUDWIG KIRCHNER *Head of a Woman*, ca. 1909

Pastel on cardboard, 34.5 x 43 cm. Solomon R. Guggenheim Museum, New York

Estate of Karl Nierendorf, By purchase 48.1172.431

HENRI MATISSE *Nude in a Forest* (*Nu dans un paysage ensoleillé*), Cavalière, 1909–12

Oil on canvas, 41.9 x 32.4 cm. Solomon R. Guggenheim Museum, New York 84.3252

FRANTIŠEK KUPKA *Planes by Colors, Large Nude* (*Plans par couleurs, grand nu*), 1909–10
Oil on canvas, 150.2 x 180.7 cm. Solomon R. Guggenheim Museum, New York
Gift, Mrs. Andrew P. Fuller 68.1860

VASILY KANDINSKY *Landscape with Factory Chimney* (*Landschaft mit Fabrikschornstein*), 1910

Oil on canvas, 66.2 x 82 cm. Solomon R. Guggenheim Museum, New York

Solomon R. Guggenheim Founding Collection, By gift 41.504

ROBERT DELAUNAY *Eiffel Tower with Trees* (*Tour Eiffel aux arbres*), summer 1910

Oil on canvas, 126.4 x 92.8 cm. Solomon R. Guggenheim Museum, New York

Solomon R. Guggenheim Founding Collection 46.1035

UMBERTO BOCCIONI Study for *The City Rises* (Studio per *La città che sale*), 1910
Oil on cardboard, 33 x 47 cm. Gianni Mattioli Collection, on long-term loan
to the Peggy Guggenheim Collection, Venice

MARC CHAGALL *Portrait of the Artist's Sister Aniuta*, 1910

Oil on canvas, 92.3 x 70.3 cm. Solomon R. Guggenheim Museum, New York

Estate of Karl Nierendorf, By purchase 48.1172.91

ALEXEI JAWLENSKY *Helene with Colored Turban (Helene mit buntem Turban)*, 1910

Oil on board, 94.2 x 81 cm. Solomon R. Guggenheim Museum, New York 65.1773.R

PIET MONDRIAN *Summer, Dune in Zeeland* (*Zomer, Duin in Zeeland*), 1910

Oil on canvas, 134 x 195 cm. Solomon R. Guggenheim Museum, New York, on permanent loan from the Gemeentemuseum den Haag, Netherlands L149.75. © 2011 Mondrian/Holtzman Trust c/o HCR International Virginia

1911

JANUARY **Vasily Kandinsky** and **Franz Marc** meet for the first time. They soon attend an Arnold Schoenberg concert; Kandinsky begins corresponding with the Viennese composer later this year. • Walter Gropius is commissioned to build the Fargus factory in Alfeld an der Leine, Germany; it becomes a prototype of modern industrial architecture. • Francesco Balilla Pratella issues the "Manifesto dei musicisti futuristi" ("Manifesto of Futurist Musicians") in Milan.

FEBRUARY **Oskar Kokoschka**'s paintings, disparaged as "massacres in paint," are included in the Hagenbund exhibition in Vienna. • **Marc** joins the Neue Künstlervereinigung München (NKVM) (New Artists' Association of Munich). • In Berlin Franz Pfemfert founds *Die Aktion* (1911–32), an Expressionist literary and political journal.

APRIL **Kazimir Malevich** and Vladimir Tatlin exhibit works at the second Soiuz molodezhi (Union of Youth) exhibition in Moscow. • Art critic and poet Guillaume Apollinaire organizes the first coherent group presentation of Cubism at the Salon des Indépendants in Paris. • Retrospective of **Henri Rousseau**'s work is included in the Salon des Indépendants. First Rousseau monograph, authored by dealer Wilhelm Uhde, is published this year. • Puteaux group is formed with **Marcel Duchamp**, **Raymond Duchamp-Villon**, **Albert Gleizes**, **Juan Gris**, **František Kupka**, **Fernand Léger**, **Jean Metzinger**, and Jacques Villon, among others.

MAY **Georges Braque** and **Pablo Picasso** participate in the Berliner Secession.

JUNE Igor Stravinsky's ballet *Petrushka* premieres in Paris. • *Im Kampf um die Kunst. Die Antwort auf den "Protest deutscher Künstler." Mit Beiträgen deutscher Künstler, Galerieleiter, Sammler und Schriftsteller* (The battle for art: The answer to "a protest of German artists," with contributions from German artists, gallery directors, collectors, and writers) from such contributors as **Kandinsky** and **Marc** as well as dealers Paul Cassirer and Uhde is published in early summer. It is a rebuttal against reactionary painter Carl Vinnen's book attacking French modernism.

Names in bold refer to artists in the exhibition.

1911

JULY **Giorgio de Chirico** arrives in Paris from Florence via Turin.

AUGUST **Braque** and **Picasso** spend the summer working side-by-side in Céret. They are later joined by **Gris**.

SEPTEMBER Apollinaire is implicated (but later exonerated) in the theft of Leonardo da Vinci's *Mona Lisa* (ca. 1503–06) from the Musée du Louvre in Paris.

OCTOBER Salon d'Automne features Cubist works by the Puteaux group. Apollinaire reviews the presentation in the newspaper *L'intransigeant*. • Moderne Kunstkring (Modern Art Circle) presents its inaugural exhibition at the Stedelijk Museum in Amsterdam and includes works by **Braque**, **Paul Cézanne**, **Piet Mondrian**, and **Picasso**. • Schoenberg arrives in Berlin from Vienna via Munich.

NOVEMBER **Umberto Boccioni** and **Carlo Carrà** visit Paris on an invitation from **Gino Severini**, who has been working there since 1906. • **Henri Matisse** travels to Russia and oversees the installation of Sergei Shchukin's French art collection in Moscow.

DECEMBER **Kandinsky**, August Macke, **Marc**, and Gabriele Münter leave the NKVM and officially found Der Blaue Reiter (The Blue Rider). Its premier exhibition opens at the Moderne Galerie Heinrich Thannhauser in Munich. • **Kandinsky**'s *Über das Geistige in der Kunst. Insbesondere in der Malerei* (*On the Spiritual in Art: And Painting in Particular*) is published in Munich, though dated 1912. • Tatlin organizes a teaching studio called Tovjer (The Tower) in Moscow. • Members of Die Brücke (The Bridge) leave the Neue Secession. The group spends more time in Berlin than in its Dresden base. • **Mondrian** arrives in Paris from Amsterdam in winter 1911–12. • This year **Otto Gutfreund**, Emil Filla, and others found in Prague the Skupina výtvarných umělců (Group of Plastic Artists), which positions itself close to the French Cubists and the Brücke. The group establishes the journal *Umělecký měsíčnik* (1911–14). • Jean Arp cofounds Der Moderner Bund (The Modern Group) in Switzerland this year.

Pages 60–61: Members of Der Blaue Reiter (The Blue Rider) on the porch of Ainmillerstraße 36, Munich, ca. 1911–12 (detail); from left: Maria and Franz Marc, Bernhard Koehler, Vasily Kandinsky (seated), Heinrich Campendonk, and Thomas von Hartmann. Photo: Gabriele Münter

EMILY D. BILSKI

CREATING A PLATFORM FOR ARTISTS: HEINRICH THANNHAUSER AND THE MODERNE GALERIE

In the last weeks of 1911, the first Der Blaue Reiter (The Blue Rider) exhibition opened at the Moderne Galerie Heinrich Thannhauser in Munich (fig. 9). Here Franz Marc's *Yellow Cow* (*Gelbe Kuh*, p. 75) first leapt into public view, and Robert Delaunay's *The City* (*La ville*, p. 77) was introduced to Germany. Both works had been painted that year, offering Munich audiences examples of the newest art, both local and international. This landmark exhibition in the history of the avant-garde[1] featured like-minded artists banding together to exhibit and eventually—in *Der Blaue Reiter* (*The Blaue Reiter Almanac*)—publish their ideas. A seminal event of 1911, the show also highlighted the role of gallery owners in the history of modernism, those art dealers who provided spaces for contemporary artists to show and sell their works and thus make their case directly to the public. Heinrich Thannhauser (fig. 11) was one of the leading dealers in Germany who played a role in furthering the great upheaval initiated by the Blaue Reiter and other avant-garde artists in the prewar period.

Thannhauser was born in a small southern German village but as a boy came to Munich, where he started out as a merchant: he sold women's ready-made clothing and owned a lighting business.[2] In 1905, together with Franz Josef Brakl, a former opera singer, he opened an art gallery that dealt primarily in the works of Munich-based artists who were associated with the Secession, though they exhibited more adventurous fare on at least one occasion: the gallery presented the first Vincent van Gogh retrospective in Germany, which was held in 1908 in cooperation with Paul Cassirer in Berlin and the artist's estate.[3] Though a conspicuous commercial failure, the exhibition had a demonstrable impact on artists. The painter Alexei Jawlensky bought (in installments) one of the only two works sold,[4] and the exhibition proved an important influence on the Munich artists who would later comprise the Blaue Reiter.[5]

In November 1909, Thannhauser dissolved his partnership with Brakl and opened the Moderne Galerie in the Arco Palais at Theatinerstraße 7. It was later described by Vasily Kandinsky as "perhaps the most beautiful exhibition space in all of Munich."[6] The ground floor boasted a spectacular skylit atrium of nearly 250 square meters, from which visitors could take a private elevator to the third floor. There, a sequence of nine rooms unfolded—music room, living room, study, and so on—simulating the "intimate living spaces"[7] that might be found in the "home of an art lover."[8] The first Blaue Reiter exhibition would be installed in these rooms, which explains some of the distinctive features visible in the iconic photographs of the exhibition, such as the domestic scale, the curious room numbers painted on the white door frames, and the small tables that sit in each room.[9] The combination of spaces both grand and intimate provided Thannhauser with great flexibility in mounting shows, often several at one time, and he embarked on an ambitious program, creating a private Kunsthalle.

The Moderne Galerie decisively shaped the artistic landscape of Munich, a city that had been retreating into a hermetic provincialism in the first years of the century. Together with his son, Justin, Thannhauser organized or hosted an array of groundbreaking exhibitions of modern and avant-garde art, including the French Impressionists and Post-Impressionists, the Italian Futurists (1912), and Pablo Picasso's first retrospective (1913, fig. 10).[10] (*Woman Ironing* [*La repasseuse*, spring 1904, p. 39], a work that Justin Thannhauser later owned, was included in the Picasso show.) Many of these exhibitions were co-organized with Germany's leading dealers, such as Cassirer, Alfred Flechtheim, and Herwarth Walden, as well as Parisian dealers Bernheim-Jeune, Durand-Ruel, Daniel-Henry Kahnweiler, and Ambroise Vollard.

Shortly after its opening, the Moderne Galerie published a lavish catalogue that included a declaration of Thannhauser's artistic credo: "It is surprising that . . . the German art trade has remained generally conservative, and that it is not willing to grant full appreciation to the products of the new art. Here the 'Moderne Galerie' shall not go along. . . . [It] will draw into its sphere of interest all that is fresh, powerful, authentic, modern in the best sense."[11] Before long, his assertion was tested when the Neue Künstlervereinigung München (NKVM) (New Artists' Association of Munich), led by Kandinsky, was looking for a venue for its first exhibition

Fig. 9 *Die erste Ausstellung der Redaktion Der Blaue Reiter* (*First Exhibition of the Blaue Reiter Editorial Office*, Moderne Galerie Heinrich Thannhauser, Munich, December 18, 1911–January 3, 1912); Franz Marc's *Yellow Cow* (*Gelbe Kuh*, 1911, p. 75) and Robert Delaunay's *The City* (*La ville*, 1911, p. 77) are partially visible. Photo: Gabriele Münter

in December 1909. Members included Adolf Erbslöh, Jawlensky, Alexander Kanoldt, Alfred Kubin, Gabriele Münter, and Marianne von Werefkin. Hugo von Tschudi, whose conflicts with the kaiser over modern art ended his tenure as a museum director in Berlin, had recently moved to Munich to become director general of the Bayerische Staatsgemäldesammlungen (Bavarian State Painting Collections); according to Kandinsky, Tschudi's "idealistic power persuaded Thannhauser to perform a truly 'heroic' act. He soon regretted and perhaps cursed this heroism."[12] Kandinsky was referring to the hostile public response to the exhibition hosted by Thannhauser, yet the gallerist did not seem to hesitate to present the second NKVM show (September 1–14, 1910). Far more ambitious, this exhibition proved to be "one of the first large group shows of the European avant-garde"[13] and included works by Georges Braque, André Derain, Henri Le Fauconnier, Picasso, Georges Rouault, and Maurice de Vlaminck, alongside Russian artists David and Vladimir Burliuk, and the local Munich artists. Kandinsky's monumental *Composition II* (*Komposition II*, 1910), which was destroyed in World War II (compare Sketch for *Composition II* [Skizze für *Komposition II*], 1909–10, p. 43), was a focal point of the presentation.

Once again, the critics were brutal, and though some NKVM members complained that Thannhauser did not adequately rise to their defense, they appreciated that "no other venue is as worthy of this event."[14] Maximilian Karl Rohe, who had written positively about the gallery's previous exhibitions, wrote: "There are only two possible ways to explain this absurd exhibition: either one assumes that the majority of the members and guests of the Association are incurably insane, or else that one deals here with brazen bluffers who know the desire for sensation of our time only too well and are trying to make use of this boom."[15] This mocking critique in particular inspired Marc to write a counterreview, which was eventually published in a brochure with Rohe's text: "People react as if we were dealing with isolated excrescences in a few sick brains, when in fact [the artworks] are the simple and austere initial forays into virgin territory. Do they not know that in every corner of Europe today, the same fresh creative spirit is active,

Fig. 10 Title page of the exhibition catalogue *Pablo Picasso* (Moderne Galerie Heinrich Thannhauser, February 1913), with typed note from Justin K. Thannhauser

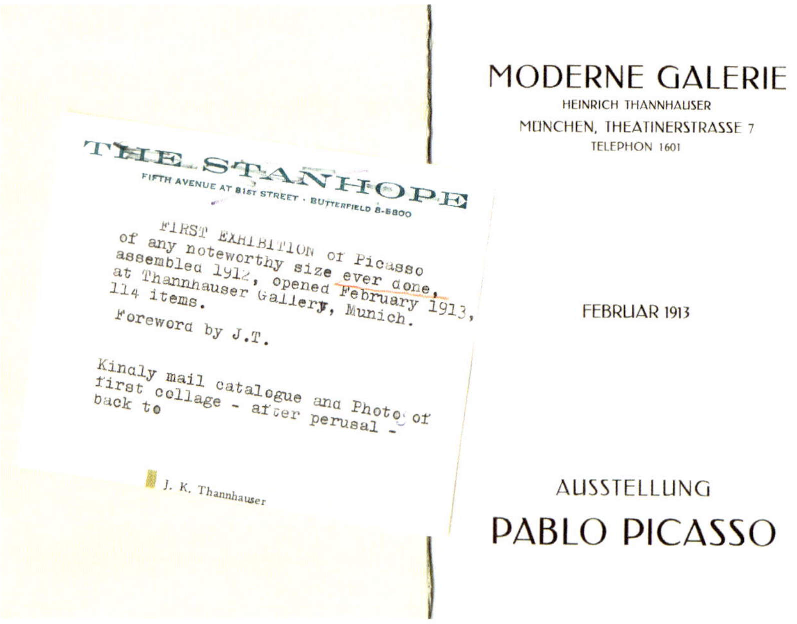

Fig. 11 Max Oppenheimer, *Portrait of Heinrich Thannhauser* (*Bildnis Heinrich Thannhauser*), 1911–12. Oil on canvas, 100 x 80 cm. Pinakothek der Moderne, Bayerische Staatsgemäldesammlungen, Munich

defiant and self-aware?"[16] Marc urged Thannhauser to put him in touch with the NKVM, and he met many of its members. As Kandinsky was in Moscow and Odessa, exhibiting his works and visiting his family, the two artists were not introduced until January 1911; the following month Marc joined the NKVM and became Kandinsky's friend and collaborator. Several of Marc's works were included in the national tour of the group's second exhibition, including *White Bull* (*The Bull*) (*Der Stier*, 1911, p. 74). In May 1911, Thannhauser mounted a two-person show of Marc and French artist (and NKVM member) Pierre Girieud.

A third NKVM exhibition was planned for December 1911; however by that time, internal disagreements between the avant-garde and more conservative members had precipitated a split, and Kandinsky, Kubin, Marc, and Münter resigned from the group. Marc and Kandinsky hastily organized an alternative exhibition, *Die erste Ausstellung der Redaktion Der Blaue Reiter* (*First Exhibition of the Blaue Reiter Editorial Office*), which they named after the almanac they had been working on together and that would be published in spring 1912. The Blaue Reiter show (December 18, 1911–January 1, 1912, and extended to January 3), which Thannhauser presented concurrently with the NKVM in adjacent rooms, included works that embodied Kandinsky's and Marc's spiritual ideas and metaphysical bent. The exhibition brought Henri Rousseau's art to Germany for the first time; a wreath hanging beneath one of his paintings referred to the artist's recent death and the esteem in which he was held (fig. 9). The French avant-garde venerated Rousseau, whose works were acquired by Delaunay and Picasso. Kandinsky wrote to Delaunay that he was "struck by the expressive power of the great poet"[17] and eager to purchase a work himself; he eventually bought two paintings with Delaunay's assistance. (Seven

Rousseau works were later reproduced in *The Blaue Reiter Almanac.*) Delaunay's paintings, which greatly influenced many German artists, among them Paul Klee and Marc, were also showcased in both the exhibition and almanac.[18] After Munich, the Blaue Reiter show traveled around Germany; its last venue was Berlin, where a version was part of the first exhibition at Walden's Der Sturm gallery that opened in March 1912.

Münter's condescending remark (in an early 1912 letter to Marc and his wife Maria) that the Blaue Reiter group (pp. 60–61) was beholden to Thannhauser for the opportunity to present the exhibition, "even though he does not know what he is doing,"[19] was in keeping with the group's perception that Thannhauser was not personally enthusiastic about their art and ideas, or worse, that he was incapable of understanding them. Thannhauser's presentation of the Italian Futurists in autumn 1912 was another occasion where his motivations were called into question. No doubt, the sensationalism of the Futurist project was an incentive for Thannhauser, who showed time and again his instinct for publicity, and the Futurists' commitment to a public role for art must have resonated with him as he shaped the goals of the Moderne Galerie and honed its public image. Perhaps Thannhauser was paying the Futurists subtle homage when he took out a notice in the newspaper announcing that the exhibition was taking place "without the responsibility of Herr Thannhauser, who has only provided his atrium [for this purpose],"[20] but it was interpreted as a lack of support for the art he showed. In his diary, Klee mocked Thannhauser for this disclaimer.[21]

Thannhauser was in fact an enthusiastic supporter (and collector) of many of the artists that he showed, including Paul Cézanne, Paul Gauguin, Édouard Manet, Max Oppenheimer, Picasso, and Van Gogh. But the heart of Thannhauser's contribution to Munich and his philosophy as a gallerist was his belief in providing an exhibiting platform as a benefit to both artists and the general public, regardless of whether the art conformed to his personal taste. Even Klee acknowledged Thannhauser's importance in showing vanguard art: "Luckily, Munich has lately become a place where much is exhibited, whether Munich likes it or not."[22]

August Macke, who contributed three paintings to the 1911–12 Blaue Reiter exhibition, recognized the vital contribution of art dealers in general in teaching the public how to understand new art: "Who can give us the means to learn through seeing? Not the professors in the academy. It is far more the museum directors, the art dealers, and the art historians who can provide us with a broader field of vision."[23] Thannhauser offers a nuanced understanding of the role played by "the ideological dealer"[24] in fostering modernism. Without his readiness to open the Moderne Galerie to new art, the city's art scene, one in which such aesthetic revolutions were occurring, would have been greatly impoverished. Through the gallery's exhibition activity, Thannhauser was an agent for the exchange of ideas and the nurturing of a cosmopolitan, international modernism in Munich. He provided a valuable model for open-mindedness and the willingness to allow for a multitude of voices.

Notes

Unless otherwise indicated, all translations are by the author.

1 Bruce Altshuler, *The Avant-Garde in Exhibition: New Art in the 20th Century* (New York: Abrams, 1994), pp. 42–59.

2 See Emily D. Bilski, *The "Moderne Galerie" of Heinrich Thannhauser*, exh. cat. (Munich: Edition Minerva, 2008), p. 14.

3 Walter Feilchenfeldt, *Vincent van Gogh and Paul Cassirer, Berlin: The Reception of Van Gogh in Germany from 1901 to 1914*. Cahier Vincent 2 (Amsterdam: Rijksmuseum Vincent Van Gogh; Zwolle, Netherlands: Uitgeverij Waanders, 1988), pp. 26–29, 66–67, 146.

4 Ibid., pp. 26–29.

5 Jill Lloyd, *Vincent van Gogh and Expressionism*, exh. cat. (Ostfildern, Germany: Hatje Cantz; Amsterdam: Van Gogh Museum, 2006), pp. 76–98.

6 Klaus Lankheit, ed., *Franz Marc im Urteil seiner Zeit* (Cologne: DuMont Schauberg, 1960), p. 46.

7 *Eröffnungs-Ausstellung November 1909*, exh. brochure (Munich: Moderne Galerie Heinrich Thannhauser, 1909), not paginated.

8 *Frankfurter Zeitung*, November 23, 1909, cited in *Moderne Galerie Heinrich Thannhauser München*, exh. cat. (Munich: Moderne Galerie Heinrich Thannhauser, 1909), p. 41.

9 Ibid., pp. 12–13.

10 For a year-by-year account of the Moderne Galerie's exhibitions, see the articles by Karl-Heinz Meissner and Mario-Andreas von Lüttichau as well as the Dokumentation in Hilmar Hoffmann, et al., *Ohne Auftrag. Zur Geschichte des Kunsthandels*, vol. 1, *München*, ed. Rupert Walser and Bernhard Wittenbrink (Munich: Walser and Wittenbrink, 1989), pp. 44–57, 117–29, and 258–261; and Bilski, *The "Moderne Galerie" of Heinrich Thannhauser*.

11 *Moderne Galerie Heinrich Thannhauser München*, pp. 4–5.

12 Lankheit, *Franz Marc im Urteil seiner Zeit*, p. 46.

13 Altshuler, *The Avant-Garde in Exhibition*, p. 45.

14 Annegret Hoberg and Helmut Friedel, eds., *Der Blaue Reiter und das Neue Bild. von der "Neuen Künstlervereinigung München" zum "Blauen Reiter,"* exh. cat. (Munich: Prestel, 1999), pp. 35–36.

15 *Münchner neueste Nachrichten*, September 10, 1910, quoted in Peter Selz, *German Expressionist Painting* (Berkeley: University of California Press, 1974), p. 196.

16 *Zwei Kritiken. Zweite Ausstellung der Neuen Künstlervereinigung München. In H. Thannhausers Moderner Galerie im Arco-Palais*, 1910; quoted in Hoberg and Friedel, *Der Blaue Reiter und das Neue Bild*, p. 37.

17 Vasily Kandinsky to Robert Delaunay, October 28, 1911, quoted in Caroline Lancher, William Rubin, et al., *Henri Rousseau* (New York: Museum of Modern Art, 1985), p. 263. See also pp. 68–69.

18 Peter-Klaus Schuster, ed., *Delaunay und Deutschland*, exh. cat. (Cologne: DuMont, 1985), pp. 72, 74.

19 Gabriele Münter to Franz and Maria Marc, quoted in Günter Herzog, "Thannhauser. Händler, Sammler, Stifter," in Heinz Holtmann, Herzog, and Brigitte Jacobs van Renswou, *Thannhauser. Händler, Sammler, Stifter*, vol. 11, *Sediment. Mitteilungen zur Geschichte des Kunsthandels* (Nuremberg: Verlag für Moderne Kunst Nürnberg, 2006), p. 11.

20 *Münchner neueste Nachrichten*, October 31, 1912, quoted in Christian Geelhaar, *Picasso. Wegbereiter und Förderer seines Aufstiegs 1899–1939* (Zurich: Palladion/ABC Verlag, 1993), p. 55.

21 Paul Klee, *Tagebücher von Paul Klee, 1898–1918*, ed. Felix Klee (Cologne: DuMont Schauberg, 1957), pp. 283–84.

22 Ibid., p. 283.

23 August Macke, in *Im Kampf um die Kunst. Die Antwort auf den "Protest deutscher Künstler." Mit Beiträgen deutscher Künstler, Galerieleiter, Sammler und Schriftsteller* (Munich: R. Piper, 1911); quoted in Dorothee Hansen, "'Preistreiberei' oder 'Brotkorbinteressen?' Kunsthandel, Preise und der Künstlerstreit 1911," in *Van Gogh "Felder." Das "Mohnfeld" und der Künstlerstreit*, ed. Wulf Herzogenrath and Dorothee Hansen, exh. cat. (Bremen: Kunsthalle Bremen, 2002), p. 191.

24 Robert Jensen, *Marketing Modernism in Fin-de-Siècle Europe* (Princeton: Princeton University Press, 1994), p. 49.

GIORGIO DE CHIRICO *The Enigma of the Hour* (*L'énigme de l'heure*), 1911

Oil on canvas, 54.9 x 71.1 cm. Private collection

VASILY KANDINSKY *Pastorale*, February 1911

Oil on canvas, 105.7 x 156.5 cm. Solomon R. Guggenheim Museum, New York

Solomon R. Guggenheim Founding Collection 45.965

FRANZ MARC *Young Boy with a Lamb* (*The Good Shepherd*) (*Knabe mit Lamm* [*Der gute Hirte*]), 1911

Oil on canvas, 88 x 83.8 cm. Solomon R. Guggenheim Museum, New York

Estate of Karl Nierendorf, By purchase 48.1172.503

FRANZ MARC *White Bull* (*The Bull*) (*Der Stier*), 1911

Oil on canvas, 100 x 135.2 cm. Solomon R. Guggenheim Museum, New York 51.1312

FRANZ MARC *Yellow Cow* (*Gelbe Kuh*), 1911

Oil on canvas, 140.5 x 189.2 cm. Solomon R. Guggenheim Museum, New York

Solomon R. Guggenheim Founding Collection 49.1210

ROBERT DELAUNAY *The City* (*La ville*), 1911

Oil on canvas, 145 x 112 cm. Solomon R. Guggenheim Museum, New York

Solomon R. Guggenheim Founding Collection, By gift 38.464

ROBERT DELAUNAY *Eiffel Tower* (*Tour Eiffel*), 1911 (dated 1910 by the artist)

Oil on canvas, 202 x 138.4 cm. Solomon R. Guggenheim Museum, New York

Solomon R. Guggenheim Founding Collection, By gift 37.463

ROBERT DELAUNAY *Red Eiffel Tower* (*La tour rouge*), 1911–12

Oil on canvas, 125 x 90.3 cm. Solomon R. Guggenheim Museum, New York

Solomon R. Guggenheim Founding Collection 46.1036

PABLO PICASSO *Accordionist* (*L'Accordéoniste*), Céret, summer 1911

Oil on canvas, 130.2 x 89.5 cm. Solomon R. Guggenheim Museum, New York

Solomon R. Guggenheim Founding Collection, By gift 37.537

PABLO PICASSO *Landscape at Céret* (*Paysage de Céret*), Céret, summer 1911

Oil on canvas, 65.1 x 50.3 cm. Solomon R. Guggenheim Museum, New York

Solomon R. Guggenheim Founding Collection, By gift 37.538

PABLO PICASSO *Bottles and Glasses* (*Bouteilles et verres*), Paris, winter 1911–12

Oil on paper, mounted on canvas, 64.4 x 49.5 cm. Solomon R. Guggenheim Museum, New York

Solomon R. Guggenheim Founding Collection, By gift 38.539

JUAN GRIS *Houses in Paris* (*Maisons à Paris*), 1911

Oil on canvas, 52.4 x 34.2 cm. Solomon R. Guggenheim Museum, New York

Estate of Karl Nierendorf, By purchase 48.1172.33

ROBERT DELAUNAY *Window on the City No. 3* (*La fenêtre sur la ville no. 3*), 1911–12

Oil on canvas, 113.7 x 130.8 cm. Solomon R. Guggenheim Museum, New York

Solomon R. Guggenheim Founding Collection 47.878.R

FRANTIŠEK KUPKA Study related to *Amorpha, Fugue in Two Colors* (*Amorpha, Fugue à deux couleurs*)
and *Amorpha, Warm Chromatic* (*Amorpha, Chromatique chaude*), 1911–12
Pastel on paper, 21.1 x 22.6 cm. Solomon R. Guggenheim Museum, New York
Gift, Mr. and Mrs. Alexander Liberman 74.2123

MARC CHAGALL *The Soldier Drinks* (*Le soldat boit*), 1911–12

Oil on canvas, 109.2 x 94.6 cm. Solomon R. Guggenheim Museum, New York

Solomon R. Guggenheim Founding Collection 49.1211

FERNAND LÉGER *The Smokers* (*Les fumeurs*), December 1911–January 1912

Oil on canvas, 129.2 x 96.5 cm. Solomon R. Guggenheim Museum, New York

Solomon R. Guggenheim Founding Collection, By gift 38.521

MARCEL DUCHAMP *Apropos of Little Sister* (*A propos de jeune soeur*), October 1911

Oil on canvas, 73 x 60 cm. Solomon R. Guggenheim Museum, New York 71.1944

MARCEL DUCHAMP *Nude (Study), Sad Young Man on a Train*
(*Nu [esquisse], jeune homme triste dans un train*), 1911–12
Oil on cardboard, 100 x 73 cm. The Solomon R. Guggenheim Foundation
Peggy Guggenheim Collection, Venice 76.2553.9

PIET MONDRIAN *Still Life with Gingerpot I* (*Stilleven met gemberpot I*), 1911

Oil on canvas, 65.5 x 75 cm. Solomon R. Guggenheim Museum, New York, on permanent loan from the Gemeentemuseum den Haag, Netherlands L295.76. © 2011 Mondrian/Holtzman Trust c/o HCR International Virginia

AMEDEO MODIGLIANI *Head* (*Tête*), 1911–13

Limestone, 71.8 x 18.4 x 20.6 cm. Solomon R. Guggenheim Museum, New York 55.1421

1912

JANUARY Proclamation of the Republic of China headed by Sun Yat-sen ends the Manchu Qing dynasty on January 1. • Burliuk brothers (David, Nikolai, and Vladimir) organize in Moscow the second Bubnovyi valet (Jack of Diamonds) exhibition without **Mikhail Larionov**. It features Western modernists such as the French Cubists (including **Pablo Picasso**), Die Brücke (The Bridge), and Der Blaue Reiter (The Blue Rider). • First exhibition of the Skupina výtvarných umělců (Group of Plastic Artists) opens at Prague's town hall.

FEBRUARY *Les peintres futuristes italiens* (*The Italian Futurist Painters*), the first presentation of Futurist painting outside of Italy, is held at the Bernheim-Jeune gallery in Paris and travels throughout Europe. • Galeries Barbazanges, Paris, stages **Robert Delaunay**'s first major exhibition. • Second Blaue Reiter exhibition opens at Galerie Hans Goltz, Munich; the German Expressionists are shown alongside, among others, Der Moderner Bund (The Modern Group) painters from Switzerland; French artists **André Derain**, Roger de La Fresnaye, and Maurice de Vlaminck; and Russian artists **Natalia Goncharova**, **Larionov**, and **Kazimir Malevich**.

MARCH First parachute jump from an airplane occurs in the United States. • **Goncharova** and **Larionov** stage the first exhibition of Oslinyi khvost (Donkey's Tail), an association they formed in 1911, at Moscow's Stroganov Art Institute. • Herwarth Walden opens Der Sturm gallery in Berlin with a show dedicated to the Blaue Reiter. • **Alexander Archipenko** exhibits at the Salon des Indépendants with the Cubists, and his sculpture atelier opens in Paris this year.

APRIL *RMS Titanic*, then the largest ocean liner ever built, sinks during its maiden voyage with over 1,500 fatalities. • **Umberto Boccioni** writes the "Manifesto tecnico della scultura futurista" ("Technical Manifesto of Futurist Sculpture") in Milan. • Guillaume Apollinaire's "La peinture nouvelle: notes d'art" ("The New Painting: Art Notes") is published in Paris.

MAY *Sonderbund Internationale Kunst-Ausstellung* (*Sonderbund International Art Exhibition*) opens in Cologne. • *Der Blaue Reiter* (*The Blaue Reiter Almanac*), edited by **Vasily Kandinsky** and **Franz Marc**, is published in Munich.

Names in bold refer to artists in the exhibition.

AUGUST **Delaunay** writes two theoretical essays this summer and fall: "La lumière" ("Light") and "Note sur la construction de la réalité de la peinture pure" ("Note on the Construction of the Reality of Pure Painting").

SEPTEMBER **Picasso** has begun incorporating collage elements, and **Georges Braque** invents papier collé; Synthetic Cubism develops.

OCTOBER War breaks out between the Balkan League (Bulgaria, Greece, Montenegro, and Serbia) and the Ottoman Empire, which relinquishes control of the Balkans. Filippo Tommaso Marinetti acts as a war correspondent. • Wilhelm Uhde organizes an **Henri Rousseau** retrospective at Bernheim-Jeune. • Walden stages **Kandinsky**'s first solo show at Der Sturm. The artist later receives a major retrospective at Galerie Hans Goltz during winter 1912–13. • Salon d'Automne and Salon de la Section d'Or open in Paris. The latter exhibition, presented at the Galerie de la Boétie and mainly organized by members of the Puteaux group, focuses exclusively on Cubism and travels throughout Europe. At a related lecture, Apollinaire coins the term "Orphism" to describe the works of **Delaunay**, **Marcel Duchamp**, **Fernand Léger**, and Francis Picabia. • August Macke and **Marc** visit **Delaunay**'s Paris studio. • Arnold Schoenberg's *Pierrot lunaire*, an Expressionist composition based on twenty-one poems by Albert Giraud, premieres in Berlin. • **Albert Gleizes** and **Jean Metzinger**'s *Du "cubisme"* (*On "Cubism"*) is published in Paris.

NOVEMBER Triple Alliance between Austria-Hungary, Italy, and Germany is renewed in Vienna on December 5. • **Larionov** shows his first Rayist works with the Soiuz molodezhi (Union of Youth) in Saint Petersburg. • André Salmon's *La jeune peinture française* (*Young French Painting*), which includes a chapter on the history of Cubism, is published in Paris.

DECEMBER Vladimir Mayakovsky's first poems are published in Moscow in *Poshchechina obshchestvennomu vkusu* (*A Slap in the Face of Public Taste*), which includes the Hylaea group's Cubo-Futurist manifesto.

Pages 94–95: The Futurists in Paris in February 1912 for the opening of *Les peintres futuristes italiens* (*The Italian Futurist Painters*, Bernheim-Jeune & cie, Paris, February 5–24, 1912); from left: Luigi Russolo, Carlo Carrà, Filippo Tommaso Marinetti, Umberto Boccioni, and Gino Severini

MILTON A. COHEN

ARTISTS WRITE! MANIFESTOS AND BOOKS IN 1912

Arnold Schoenberg's *Pierrot lunaire*, Pablo Picasso's and Georges Braque's first collages and papier collés, abstractions by Robert Delaunay and František Kupka, and several landmark art exhibitions—these made 1912 a banner year of prewar modernism. It also marked the publication of several important documents by the modernist groups that were proliferating so rapidly in the early twentieth century. The Italian Futurists, who issued more than fifty manifestos in all, published "Les exposants au public" ("The Exhibitors to the Public") in February 1912 to accompany the Paris opening of their new exhibition (pp. 94–95). That same year, two manifestos appeared, declaring the liberation of words and syllables from traditional syntax: Filippo Tommaso Marinetti's "Manifesto tecnico della letteratura futurista" ("Technical Manifesto of Futurist Literature"), which led directly to his 1914 book *Zang Tumb Tumb. Adrianopoli, Ottobre 1912* (Zang Tumb Tumb. Adrianople, October 1912, fig. 12), and the Russian Cubo-Futurists' *Poshchechina obshchestvennomu vkusu* (*A Slap in the Face of Public Taste*), which argued for the "self-sufficient word," anticipating transrational "zaum" poetry of 1913. Larger publications also achieved prominence, such as *Der Blaue Reiter* (*The Blaue Reiter Almanac*), edited by Vasily Kandinsky and Franz Marc, and *Du "cubisme"* (*On "Cubism"*) by Albert Gleizes and Jean Metzinger, the first scholarly discussion of the movement (fig. 13). This frenetic urge to publish statements may seem odd, especially for painters more facile with oils than words. But the writings inevitably issued from the groups to which these artists belonged—ones eager to state their aesthetic program and philosophic positions, not least in order to compete with other groups. Of these artist-authored publications, "The Exhibitors to the Public" and *The Blaue Reiter Almanac* are among the most important and effectively demonstrate the range of ambitions and aesthetics of these documents.

"The Exhibitors" is an amalgam of cheeky declarations, explication of a major Futurist principle (force lines), and justification of a more emotive, subjective use of line expressing "the simultaneousness of states of mind."[1] Appearing almost two years after the Futurists' "Manifesto tecnico della pittura futurista" ("Technical Manifesto of Futurist Painting," 1910), with its emphasis on dynamism and the interpenetration of bodies with surrounding spaces, the 1912 manifesto states: "Every object reveals by its lines how it would resolve itself were it to follow the tendencies of its forces. . . . [E]very object influences its neighbor, not by reflections of light . . . but by a real competition of lines and by real conflicts of planes, following the emotional law which governs the picture."[2] Realized fully, these "force lines" were intended to "decompose" and extrapolate objects into vectors of motion and conflict. Significantly, they were as applicable to abstract shapes and lines—the direction all Futurist painting was headed—as to recognizable figures in conflict.

The new manifesto also develops the technical manifesto's concept of interpenetrating outsides and insides, the subject and its environment, while adding a temporal and subjective dimension, the simultaneity of states of mind: "the picture must be a synthesis of *what one remembers and of what one sees*." This idea applies directly to the *States of Mind* (*Stato d'animo*) paintings that Umberto Boccioni, the manifesto's chief author, had completed in late 1911 and was showing at the exhibition.[3]

Beyond heralding their aesthetic innovations, the Futurists declare in no uncertain terms that they are now "at the head of the European movement in painting." While the Cubists

Fig. 12 Filippo Tommaso Marinetti, *Zang Tumb Tumb. Adrianopoli, Ottobre 1912* (Zang Tumb Tumb. Adrianople, October 1912). Published by Edizioni Futuriste de "Poesia," Milan, 1914. Page (irreg.): 20.4 x 13.5 cm. The Museum of Modern Art, New York, Gift of The Judith Rothschild Foundation (Boris Kerdimun Archive)

"obstinately continue to paint objects motionless, frozen, and all the static aspects of Nature, . . . [we] seek for a style of motion" that represents the future.[4] As intended, such provocations got under the skin of competitive leaders like Guillaume Apollinaire, who championed the Cubists and now felt compelled (in his review of the Futurists' 1912 exhibition) to belittle these upstarts for their "insolence that might aptly be called ignorance" and "sheer idiocy."[5] Such sniping, however, only played into the Futurists' hands by calling more attention to them.

The Blaue Reiter Almanac differs sharply from "The Exhibitors" in size, scope, and aesthetics. The almanac was the idea of two Munich-based painters, Kandinsky and Marc (fig. 14), though its nineteen articles and essays (not to mention its 144 reproductions) required the participation of artists and theorists from many countries and periods. Kandinsky and Marc held strong views about where not only their art, but also all avant-garde styles of the early 1910s were headed: toward a new age of spirituality to replace an era of smug materialism and philistinism. Further, the two painters were determined to make their new movement, Der Blaue Reiter (The Blue Rider), a kind of nexus of these new styles and groups and the embodiment of the two painters' ecumenical and spiritual ideas about art. Even before they had left the Neue Künstlervereinigung München (NKVM) (New Artists' Association of Munich) in December 1911, the two had already begun organizing their own group that previous summer.[6] The first Blaue Reiter exhibition, held in December 1911, included painters from Paris (Delaunay, Henri Le Fauconnier, and the late Henri Rousseau), Vienna (Schoenberg), and Russia (David and Vladimir Burliuk), as well as several from Germany, to realize the organizers' aim of showing "the multiplicity of ways through which the inner wishes of artists take shape."[7]

Fig. 13 Albert Gleizes and Jean Metzinger, title page of *Du "cubisme"* (*On "Cubism"*). Published by Eugène Figuière et cie, Paris, 1912

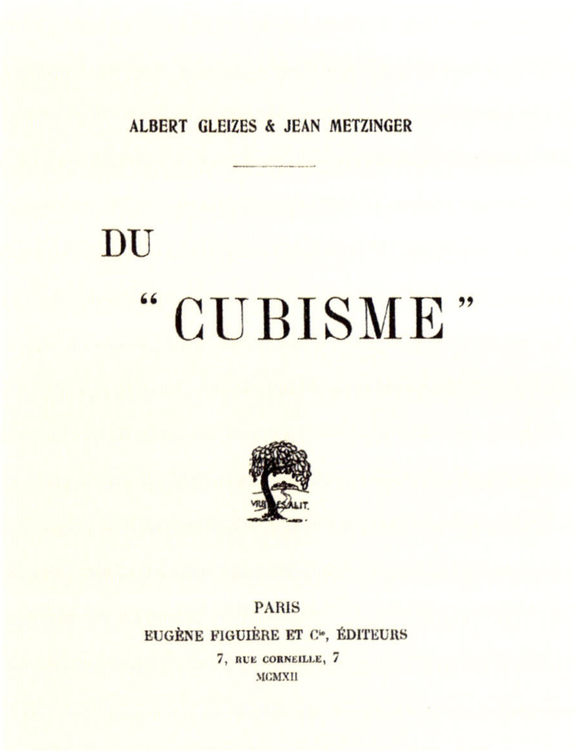

ALBERT GLEIZES & JEAN METZINGER

DU

"CUBISME"

PARIS

EUGÈNE FIGUIÈRE ET Cie, ÉDITEURS

7, RUE CORNEILLE, 7

MCMXII

Fig. 14 Franz Marc and Vasily Kandinsky with the cover woodcut for *Der Blaue Reiter* (*The Blaue Reiter Almanac*, 1912) on the porch of Ainmillerstraße 36, Munich. Photo: Gabriele Münter

Not content with just mounting exhibitions, Kandinsky and Marc, with the close collaboration of August Macke, planned to publish a collection of articles and art reproductions in a volume that could effectively promulgate their ideas and "show that something was happening *everywhere*," as Kandinsky put it.[8] The new almanac, Kandinsky wrote to Marc at the outset, must be "a link to the past as well as a ray to the future. . . . We will put an Egyptian work beside a small Zeh [children's art], a Chinese work beside a Rousseau, a folk print beside a Picasso. . . . Eventually we will attract poets and musicians."[9] In his preface to the second edition, Marc recalled: "With a divining rod we searched through the art of the past and present."[10] As art historian Klaus Lankheit notes, "the pictures were carefully placed in relation to each other so that the 'inner sound' of one picture would be answered by the 'contrasting sound' of the other."[11] As these ambitions reflect, the editors were determined to remove barriers separating "high" art from folk art, "primitive" from Western art, ancient from modern, while emphasizing that the new styles were truly international.[12] Even the authors were to be geographically diverse, almost programmatically so. As Kandinsky wrote to Marc, "From [Thomas von] Hartmann I ordered an article on Armenian music and a music letter from Russia. . . . Schönberg *must* write on German music. Le Fauconnier *must* get a Frenchman [to write for us]. . . . Just wait! We will get a real pulse in our dear book."[13]

The published book exceeded these ambitious plans. Schoenberg not only wrote "Das Verhältnis zum Text" ("The Relationship to the Text"), but he submitted a new score, *Herzgewächse*. Alban Berg and Anton von Webern also contributed musical scores. Kandinsky wrote a semi-abstract "stage composition" synaesthetically entitled *Der gelbe Klang* (*Yellow Sound*). Articles on masks (by Macke), on Delaunay's painting, on Russian art (by David Burliuk), and on Alexander Scriabin's *Prometheus*, as well as Kandinsky's theoretical tract "Über die Formfrage" ("On the Question of Form"), were interspersed with pictures of Bavarian glass painting, fifteenth-century woodcuts, Chinese painting, Russian folk prints, and wood sculpture from South Borneo, along with reproductions of recent works by Ernst Ludwig Kirchner, Henri Matisse, Picasso, and many other modernists.

The three short articles by Marc were especially provocative. "Die 'Wilden' Deutschlands" ("The 'Savages' of Germany") begins: "In this time of the great struggle for a new art we fight like disorganized 'savages' against an old, established power. The battle seems to be unequal, but spiritual matters are never decided by numbers, only by the power of ideas."[14] In the same article, Marc notes an essential difference between these Germanic "savages" (in this instance, the editors themselves) and French Cubists and creators of "the most beautiful prismatic colors" (probably an allusion to Delaunay): "[R]enewal must not be merely formal but in fact a rebirth of thinking. *Mysticism* was awakened in their souls and with it the most ancient elements of art. . . . [The savages aim] to create out of their work *symbols* for their own time, symbols that belong on the altars of a future spiritual religion."[15]

In sum, as Kandinsky explained in 1936, he and Marc intended the almanac as "a 'synthesized' book which was to eliminate old narrow ideas and tear down the walls between the arts."[16] Of course, amid these high-minded aims, the editors strategically placed themselves at the center of this artistic ferment. As Marc wrote to his brother, "The Editors of the *Blaue Reiter* will now be the starting point for new exhibitions. . . . We will try to become the center of the modern movement."[17] In so doing, they were quite willing to diminish the influence of some rival groups. For instance, when Marc wanted to feature in the almanac the art of Die Brücke (The Bridge), Kandinsky responded: "I think it is incorrect to immortalize them in the *document* of our modern art . . . or as a more or less decisive, leading factor. At any rate, I am against [giving them] *large* reproductions. . . . The small reproduction means: this *too* is being done. The large one: *this* is being done."[18]

Although these sample writings from artists in 1912 differ radically in style and scope, they both express salient features of prewar modernism. The distinctive frisson of aesthetic seriousness and competitive jockeying for prominence—self-evident in "The Exhibitors" but concealed beneath the almanac's idealism—characterized virtually all modernist groups before the war. A subjective, intuitive dimension of modernism also informs both documents: it is central to Kandinsky's and Marc's belief in the new spirituality of art, but also present in the Futurists' concept of simultaneity as "states of mind," which, expressed by dynamic force lines, give "the emotional ambience of a picture."[19] In turn, this subjectivity, so central to Germanic modernism,[20] counterpoints the "objective," analytical mentality typical of Cubism—and French modernism generally, as painters like Delaunay would argue[21]—to effect the complementary sides of prewar modernism.

Notes

1 Umberto Boccioni, Carlo D. Carrà, Luigi Russolo, Giacomo Balla, and Gino Severini, "The Exhibitors to the Public," in Herschel B. Chipp, *Theories of Modern Art: A Source Book by Artists and Critics* (Berkeley: University of California Press, 1968), p. 295.

2 Ibid., p. 296.

3 Ibid.

4 Ibid., p. 294.

5 Guillaume Apollinaire, *Apollinaire on Art: Essays and Reviews, 1902–1918*, ed. Leroy C. Breunig, trans. Susan Suleiman, *The Documents of 20th Century Art* (New York: Viking Press, 1972), p. 202.

6 The NKVM was increasingly divided over nonfigurative art. Vasily Kandinsky and Franz Marc angrily left the group when it refused to hang Kandinsky's *Composition V* (*Komposition V*, 1911) at its new exhibition.

7 *Die erste Ausstellung der Redaktion Der Blaue Reiter*, exh. cat., quoted in Annette Vezin and Luc Vezin, *Kandinsky and Der Blaue Reiter* (Paris: Pierre Terrail, 1992), p. 178.

8 Vasily Kandinsky to Franz Marc, September 1, 1911, quoted in Klaus Lankheit, "Introduction," in Kandinsky and Marc, eds., *The Blaue Reiter Almanac*, new documentary edition, ed. and trans. Lankheit (New York: Viking Press, 1974), p. 17 (Kandinsky's emphasis).

9 Vasily Kandinsky to Franz Marc, June 19, 1911, quoted in ibid., pp. 15–16.

10 Franz Marc, preface to *Der Blaue Reiter*, 2nd ed., quoted in ibid., p. 38.

11 Lankheit, "Introduction," p. 38.

12 This emphasis on internationalism was their direct response to the Carl Vinnen controversy in Germany, which arose when an obscure painter complained in an open letter to a newspaper that galleries and museums devoted too much space to foreign artists at the expense of German ones.

13 Kandinsky to Marc, September 1, 1911, quoted in Lankheit, "Introduction," pp. 16–17.

14 Franz Marc, "The 'Savages' of Germany," in Kandinsky and Marc, *The Blaue Reiter Almanac*, p. 61.

15 Ibid., p. 64 (Marc's emphasis).

16 Vasily Kandinsky, "Franz Marc," *Cahiers d'art* (Paris), nos. 8–10 (1936), quoted in ibid., p. 37.

17 Franz Marc to his brother, December 3, 1911, quoted in ibid., p. 14.

18 Vasily Kandinsky to Franz Marc, February 2, 1912, quoted in Lankheit, "Introduction," p. 20 (Kandinsky's emphasis).

19 Boccioni, et al., "The Exhibitors to the Public," p. 298. Elsewhere, the manifesto states: "We thus create a sort of emotive ambience, seeking by intuition the sympathies and the links which exist between the exterior (concrete) scene and the interior (abstract) emotion," p. 297.

20 For example, both Kandinsky and Arnold Schoenberg claimed that their invention in this period was driven by "inner necessity."

21 Witness Robert Delaunay's skepticism (in a 1913 letter to Marc) about the importance of the spirituality Marc and Kandinsky emphasized: "For progress in art, I find that no mysticism is needed. . . . What makes my art different from the few things I saw in your country is this enthusiasm or rather mystic daze to which the young Germans, even the most interesting ones, are subject, and which hampers and paralyzes the vital impulse." Quoted in Gustav Vriesen and Max Imdahl, *Robert Delaunay: Light and Color* (New York: Abrams, 1967), pp. 57–58.

LUIGI RUSSOLO *Solidity of Fog* (*Solidità della nebbia*), 1912
Oil on canvas, 100 x 65 cm. Gianni Mattioli Collection, on long-term loan to the Peggy Guggenheim Collection, Venice

CARLO CARRÀ Study for *The Galleria in Milan* (Studio per *La Galleria di Milano*), 1912
Graphite and charcoal on paper, 37 x 21 cm. Gianni Mattioli Collection, on long-term loan to the Peggy Guggenheim Collection, Venice

CARLO CARRÀ *The Galleria in Milan* (*La Galleria di Milano*), 1912
Oil on canvas, 91 x 51.5 cm. Gianni Mattioli Collection, on long-term loan to the Peggy Guggenheim Collection, Venice

MIKHAIL LARIONOV *Glass* (*Steklo*), 1912 (dated 1909 by the artist)

Oil on canvas, 104.1 x 97.1 cm. Solomon R. Guggenheim Museum, New York 53.1362

KAZIMIR MALEVICH *Morning in the Village after Snowstorm* (*Utro posle v'iugi v derevne*), 1912

Oil on canvas, 80 x 80 cm. Solomon R. Guggenheim Museum, New York 52.1327

VASILY KANDINSKY *Improvisation 28 (second version)* (*Improvisation 28 [zweite Fassung]*), 1912
Watercolor, india ink, and graphite on paper, 39 x 56.1 cm. The Hilla von Rebay Foundation, on extended loan to the Solomon R. Guggenheim Museum, New York 1970.127

VASILY KANDINSKY *Improvisation 28 (second version)* (*Improvisation 28 [zweite Fassung]*), 1912

Oil on canvas, 111.4 x 162.1 cm. Solomon R. Guggenheim Museum, New York

Solomon R. Guggenheim Founding Collection, By gift 37.239

ROBERT DELAUNAY *Simultaneous Windows (2nd Motif, 1st Part)*

(*Les fenêtres simultanées [2e motif, 1re partie]*), 1912

Oil on canvas, 55.2 x 46.3 cm. Solomon R. Guggenheim Museum, New York

Solomon R. Guggenheim Founding Collection, By gift 41.464

RAYMOND DUCHAMP-VILLON *Maggy*, 1912 (cast 1954)

Bronze, 74 x 33.3 x 40.6 cm, edition 3/8. Solomon R. Guggenheim Museum, New York 57.1464

CONSTANTIN BRANCUSI *Muse* (*La muse*), 1912

Marble, 45 x 23 x 17 cm. Solomon R. Guggenheim Museum, New York 85.3317

shown on: *Oak base*, 1920. Oak, 97.5 x 47.3 x 47 cm

Solomon R. Guggenheim Museum, New York 58.1516

ALBERT GLEIZES *Head in a Landscape* (*Tête dans un paysage*), 1912–13

Oil on canvas, 37.6 x 50.4 cm. Solomon R. Guggenheim Museum, New York

The Hilla Rebay Collection 71.1936.R151

JEAN METZINGER *Woman with a Fan* (*Femme à l'éventail*), ca. 1912–13

Oil on canvas, 90.7 x 64.2 cm. Solomon R. Guggenheim Museum, New York

Solomon R. Guggenheim Founding Collection, By gift 38.531

FERNAND LÉGER *Study of a Nude*, winter 1912–13

Oil on paper, 63.6 x 48.5 cm. The Solomon R. Guggenheim Foundation

Peggy Guggenheim Collection, Venice 76.2553.19

FERNAND LÉGER *Nude Model in the Studio* (*Le modèle nu dans l'atelier*), 1912–13

Oil on burlap, 128.6 x 95.9 cm. Solomon R. Guggenheim Museum, New York

Solomon R. Guggenheim Founding Collection 49.1193

1913

JANUARY Aldo Palazzeschi, Giovanni Papini, and Ardengo Soffici establish the Futurist publication *Lacerba* (1913–15) in Florence.

FEBRUARY Moderne Galerie Heinrich Thannhauser, Munich, organizes Germany's first **Pablo Picasso** retrospective. • *International Exhibition of Modern Art* (popularly known as the Armory Show) opens in New York and includes controversial works by artists such as **Marcel Duchamp**, **Vasily Kandinsky**, and **Henri Matisse**. • First issue of the *Montjoie!* gazette (1913–16), edited by Riciotto Canudo, is published in Paris.

MARCH U.S. President Woodrow Wilson is inaugurated on March 4. • Orphism receives considerable attention at the Salon des Indépendants in Paris. • *Mishen* (*Target*) exhibition opens in Moscow and includes Rayist paintings by **Natalia Goncharova** and **Mikhail Larionov** as well as works by **Kazimir Malevich**. • **Luigi Russolo** writes his manifesto "L'arte dei rumori" ("The Art of Noises") in Milan. • Guillaume Apollinaire's collection of writings, *Méditations esthétiques. Les peintres cubistes* (*The Cubist Painters: Aesthetic Meditations*), is published, followed by his collection of poems, *Alcools*, a few weeks later in Paris.

APRIL Woolworth skyscraper opens in New York as the tallest building in the world. • Marlborough Gallery, London, presents **Gino Severini**'s first solo exhibition. • Bernheim-Jeune gallery, Paris, mounts a **Matisse** exhibition. • **Larionov**'s manifesto *Luchizm* (*Rayism*) is published in Moscow.

MAY Filippo Tommaso Marinetti's *Distruzione della sintassi—Immaginazione senza fili—Parole in libertà* (*Destruction of Syntax—Wireless Imagination—Words-in-Freedom*) is published in Florence. • **Fernand Léger**'s "Les origines de la peinture contemporaine et sa valeur représentative" ("The Origins of Painting and Its Representational Value") is published in *Montjoie!* • *Le sacre du printemps* (*The Rite of Spring*, 1910–13), with music by Igor Stravinsky and choreography by Vaslav Nijinsky, premieres in Paris.

JUNE Second phase of the Balkan War begins as Bulgaria disputes territory against a coalition consisting of Greece, Serbia, Romania, and the Ottoman Empire. Bulgaria is defeated. • **Severini**'s solo show travels to Der Sturm in Berlin. • Galerie de la Boétie, Paris, stages **Umberto Boccioni**'s first sculpture exhibition. • Apollinaire writes *L'antitradition. Manifeste futuriste* (*Futurist Anti-tradition*). It is soon published in Paris and Florence.

Names in bold refer to artists in the exhibition.

1913

JULY **Goncharova** and **Larionov**'s "Luchisty i budushchniki. Manifest" ("Rayonists and Futurists: A Manifesto") is published in *Oslinyi khvost i mishen'* (Donkey's tail and target) in Moscow. • *Rheinische Expressionisten* (*Expressionists of the Rhineland*), organized by August Macke, opens at the Friedrich Cohen gallery, Bonn. • Members of London's Bloomsbury Group found the Omega Workshops.

AUGUST **Carlo Carrà**'s *La pittura dei suoni, rumori, odori* (*The Painting of Sounds, Noises, and Smells*) is published in Milan.

SEPTEMBER Erster deutscher Herbstsalon (First German Autumn Salon), a major exhibition of international vanguard art principally organized by Herwarth Walden, opens at Der Sturm. • Czech group Skupina výtvarných umělců (Group of Plastic Artists) show at Der Sturm and Galerie Hans Goltz, Munich. • In autumn, Sigmund Freud's *Totem und Tabu. Einige Übereinstimmungen im Seelenleben der Wilden und der Neurotiker* (*Totem and Taboo: Resemblances Between the Mental Lives of Savages and Neurotics*), a collection of four essays, is published in Vienna.

OCTOBER In the first moving assembly line, Ford Motors in Detroit produces the Model T, which has been on the market since 1908.

NOVEMBER Marcel Proust's *Du côté de chez Swann* (*Swann's Way*), the first volume of his magnum opus *À la recherche du temps perdu* (*A Remembrance of Things Past*), is published in Paris.

DECEMBER *Probeda nad Sointsem* (*Victory over the Sun*), the first Futurist opera with costumes and sets designed by **Malevich**, premieres in Saint Petersburg. • This year, Gabrielle "Coco" Chanel opens her first shops in Paris and in the resort town of Deauville, France. • **Malevich** produces a drawing in which he abandons recognizable subject matter entirely, thus laying the foundation for Suprematism. • Also this year, **Ernst Ludwig Kirchner**'s *Chronik der KG Brücke* (*Chronicle of the Artists' Group Brücke*), which precipitates the dissolution of Die Brücke (The Bridge), is published in Berlin.

Pages 120–21: Artists participating in the exhibition *Mishen* (*Target*, Moscow, March 24–April 7, 1913); from left: Mikhail Larionov, Maurice Fabbri, Mikhail Le-Dantyu, Natalia Goncharova, Vladimir Obolenski, and Sergei Romanovich. Reproduced in *Oslinyi khvost i mishen'* (Donkey's tail and target, Moscow, 1913)

THE SIMULTANEOUS SPACES OF 1913

TARA WARD

On July 1, 1913, the Eiffel Tower broadcast the fact that it was ten in the morning (fig. 15). That seemingly banal transmission was the result of decades of heated negotiation; it was the inaugural moment of a radical reorganization of spatial and temporal experience: standard time. Time zones are a product of 1913, and while today they most often catch our attention as a minor annoyance of travel or global communication, those lateral bands of shared time added a new geography to contemporary consciousness and helped establish the sense that time and space were ideas as well as physical realities. Suddenly, the minute hands of clocks throughout the world were synchronized (a major shift from a system in which each country, each city, and even each town could determine its own time), and thanks to this convention, it became possible to easily establish the simultaneity of events across the globe. Perhaps even more dramatic was the reorganization of world space created by standard time. Now geography could be understood not just in terms of topographical features or politics (though both had played a role in the divisions of standard time), but also according to the abstract idea that the planet was composed of twenty-four slices and that these somewhat arbitrary partitions established a direct and practical link between time and space. In short, a new picture of the world emerged, one that did not represent national boundaries or mountains. Rather, it diagrammed a theoretical concept of space conceived in terms of the entire globe and rearranged the way we live our lives.

While standard time may have been the most far-reaching abstract space created in 1913, it was far from the only one, and the pattern of lengthy study and partisan statements (see the discussion of manifestos in “Artists Write! Manifestos and Books in 1912,” pp. 98–103) blossoming into new visions of the world was repeated again and again throughout the year. In the visual arts, a proliferation of nonobjective images, imaginary worlds, and novel modes of representation was displayed to an evermore connected international audience. The year 1913 produced numerous maps of theoretical, imagined, and practical places, which showed that these spaces might all exist at the same time, a possibility that was met by both celebration and disdain.

Robert Delaunay probably produced more images of the Eiffel Tower than any other painter. The motif, which he saw as both a compositional challenge (how does one fit something that tall into the confined space of a painting?) and a symbol of the modern world, is nearly omnipresent throughout his mature work. In *Red Eiffel Tower* (*La tour rouge*, 1911–12, p. 79), the splayed scaffolding of Gustave Eiffel’s engineering marvel hovers amid a somewhat indistinguishable background of curtains, buildings, and clouds as if the city of Paris itself has been reduced to an echo

Fig. 15 Postcard with a panoramic view of Paris from the Arc de Triomphe to the Eiffel Tower, collected by Robert Delaunay

of the tower's form. Alternately in his *Windows* (*Fenêtres*) series (1912–14, p. 112), the tower is a dark shadow among the brightly colored shapes that now lack any obvious connection to the urban landscape. By 1913 Delaunay had moved into what he termed his "constructive" phase and spent much of the year working on a series of images of the sun and the moon, such as *Simultaneous Contrasts: Sun and Moon* (*Soleil, lune, simultané 2*, 1913, fig. 16). This focus on the solar system brought to the fore the circular elements that would characterize his production for the rest of his life; those orbs with their contrasting hues were his system for constructing space. In the painter's mind, these abstract forms were a way of experiencing depth. Color was central to his innovative building method in that the various combinations of hues tended to create a feeling of three-dimensionality, which Delaunay learned from his careful study of the work of the nineteenth-century color theorist Michel-Eugène Chevreul.[1] The scientist's term for some of these coloristic effects was "simultaneous contrast," and Delaunay became so obsessed with the idea that he referred to not only his own painting, but also his friends' poetry, various world cities, and even the Eiffel Tower as "simultaneous."[2]

While Delaunay was pondering celestial bodies, his wife and fellow artist Sonia Delaunay was busy sewing, turning those circular colors into dresses. Made to be worn to a dancehall in Montparnasse that she would also depict on canvas, her *Simultaneous Dress* (*Robe simultanée*, 1913, fig. 17) underlines the way that modern painting was linked to everyday spaces. The forms of the couple's singular style are rendered three-dimensional, and as Sonia Delaunay walked through the streets, they interacted with the city that had inspired them. But the space of Paris was also changing thanks to technology—Sonia said that the circular forms of her work were inspired by electric streetlights—and new urban experiences. A fad for the tango swept Paris in 1913, and that physically demanding dance combined with Paul Poiret's Ballets Russes–inspired couture led women to cast aside their corsets. Since it did not require stays, the *Simultaneous Dress* also displays a freedom of feminine movement and therefore inaugurates another new space of 1913.

While many artists such as the Delaunays, František Kupka, and Piet Mondrian wholeheartedly embraced (and even danced their way through) these new spaces, others like Fernand Léger were more interested in the way space is understood and navigated. Thanks to a contract from the dealer Daniel-Henry Kahnweiler, Léger had the financial freedom to turn away from the large-scale salon works he had been producing and spent most of 1913 on a prolonged formal investigation known as the *Contrasts of Forms* (*Contraste de formes*, 1913–14) series. In the finished example in this catalogue (p. 145), a pile of shapes in a limited set of colors confronts the viewer with ambiguous spatial clues that must be pieced together in the process of looking. The red rectangles so prominent at the left-hand side of the picture are reminiscent of the distant rooftops of *The Smokers* (*Les fumeurs*, December 1911–January 1912, p. 89); however, the uneasy relationship between these "roofs" and the white rectangles abutting them, not to mention their odd positions on the canvas, mean that the viewer must mentally arrange these

Fig. 16 Robert Delaunay, *Simultaneous Contrasts: Sun and Moon* (*Soleil, lune, simultané 2*, 1913 (dated 1912 on painting). Oil on canvas, 134.5 cm diam. The Museum of Modern Art, New York, Mrs. Simon Guggenheim Fund

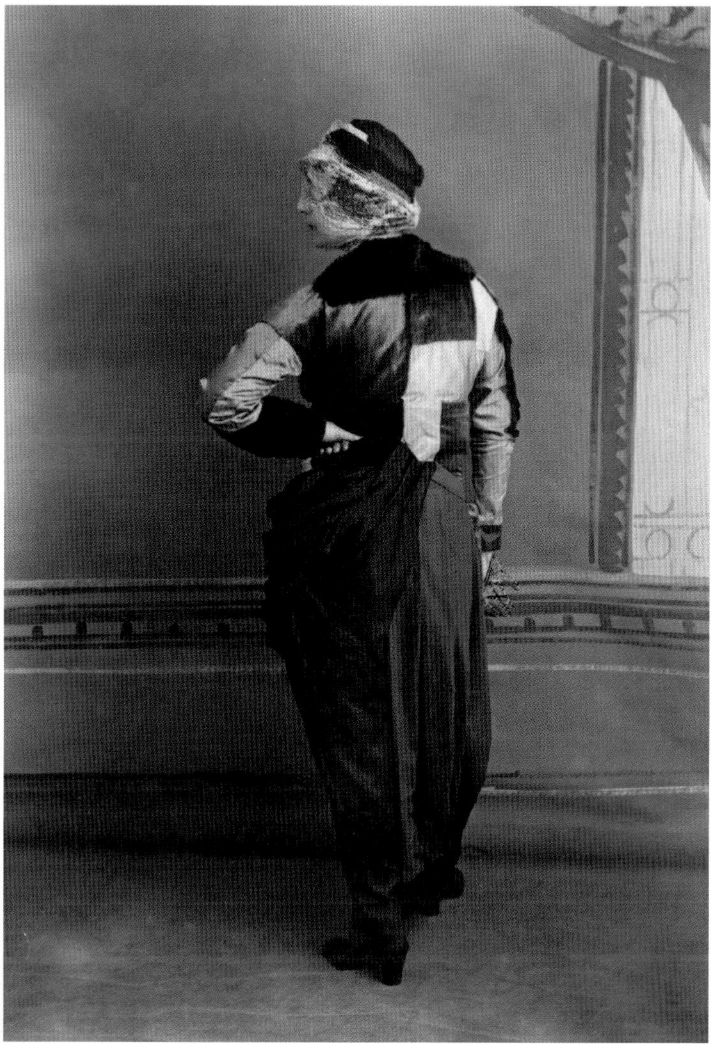

Fig. 17 Sonia Delaunay wearing a *Simultaneous Dress* (*Robe simultanée*), 1913

building block–like pieces in order to construct a sense of three-dimensional space. Similarly, the cylindrical forms at the center of *Contrast of Forms* appear rounded thanks in part to the irregular white paint that seems to evoke light on a three-dimensional surface; yet, the source of this light and the relative location of the tubes are so confusing that the viewer must determine the relationship between them by carefully pondering each form as it intersects another. This process of constructing space by placing objects side-by-side and requiring the viewer to create a mental relationship between them is what Léger meant by the term "contrast," and his sense that space is created rather than given corresponds to the explosion of different types of spaces happening at this moment.[3]

Marc Chagall's depictions of Russian peasant life appear worlds away from the Delaunays and Léger, but were in fact produced nearly side by side. When Chagall painted *The Flying Carriage* (*La calèche volante*, 1913, p. 140), he was living and working at La Ruche, an artists' compound on the southern outskirts of Paris. Created by the academic sculptor Alfred Boucher in 1901, the enclosed studio complex was always intended to provide inexpensive space for artists. To keep construction expenses to a minimum, Boucher purchased materials left over from the 1900 Exposition universelle (Universal Exposition), the world's fair held that year in Paris, including the former Bordeaux wine pavilion designed by Eiffel's firm. That iron structure became

La Ruche's main building and housed not only Chagall, but also Léger, Amedeo Modigliani, and Diego Rivera at various points during its history. Although they were not abstract, the dream worlds of Chagall and Giorgio de Chirico, who was living in Paris at this time, were also new spaces that could be simultaneously viewed alongside the changing city and nonobjective paintings.

La Ruche, like a number of Parisian enclaves, drew artists from all over the globe. The city's large international community attested to the increasing ease of transportation and communication. Exchanges between the Parisian avant-garde and its colleagues in Germany and Russia were commonplace in the early 1910s, but 1913 marked the moment that their reach extended to the New World. The *International Exhibition of Modern Art*, also known as the Armory Show, which began on February 17, 1913, in New York and then toured the United States, was the first large-scale presentation of European modern art in America. Save for those who could visit such rarefied spaces as Alfred Stieglitz's gallery at 291 Fifth Avenue, New York, Americans were unaware of the development of European art since Impressionism. Thus many were shocked by the bright colors and near abstraction of many of the over twelve hundred works on view. The wide-ranging show included works by Constantin Brancusi, Paul Gauguin, Henri Rousseau, and Vincent van Gogh, but Marcel Duchamp's *Nude Descending a Staircase, No. 2* (*Nu descendant un escalier n°2*, 1912) was the subject of particular scorn. James Townsend declared in *American Art News* that he knew of no one who could find either a woman or a staircase in Duchamp's depiction of movement, which, while the artist denied it, was undoubtedly related to the Futurists' experiments with spatial illustrations of time and force. By 1913, these innovations had culminated in such works as Giacomo Balla's *Paths of Movement + Dynamic Sequences* (*Linee andamentali + successioni dinamiche*, 1913, p. 146).[4]

While Americans were up in arms about Duchamp's 1912 work, Parisians were dealing with their own scandal. The premier of the ballet *Le sacre du printemps* (*The Rite of Spring*) on May 29, 1913, ended with the police being called to control the disconcerted crowd. Whether Igor Stravinsky's sonic dissonance or Vaslav Nijinsky's unorthodox movements caused the disturbance is still subject to debate; however, the Futurists' call for riot-causing art had been answered and the array of 1913's simultaneous spaces had created a battle for aesthetic territory. This explosion of revolutionary maps, visions, and systems was no doubt disorienting, but at least 1914 would be rung in at regular hour-long intervals progressing around the globe. It would not, however, be a happy new year.

Notes

Unless otherwise indicated, all translations are by the author.

1 M. E. Chevreul, *De la loi du contraste simultané des couleurs, et de l'assortiment des objets colorés, considéré d'après cette loi* (Paris: Pitois-Levrault et cie, 1839).

2 See Robert Delaunay, *Du cubisme à l'art abstrait*, ed. Pierre Francastel, with catalogue raisonné by Guy Habasque (Paris: S.E.V.P.E.N., 1957).

3 For a discussion of contrast and its relationship to modernity, see Fernand Léger, "Contemporary Achievements in Painting," in *Functions of Painting*, trans. Alexandra Anderson (New York: Viking Press, 1973), pp. 11–19.

4 James Townsend, "A Bomb from the Blue," *American Art News* 11, no. 20 (February 22, 1913), p. 9. A copy is available online at aaa.si.edu/collectionsonline/kuhnwalt/container228158.htm on p. 22 and also in the Walter Kuhn archives at the Smithsonian Institution, Washington, D.C., box 2, folder 34, p. 23.

FRANZ MARC *The Unfortunate Land of Tyrol* (*Das arme Land Tirol*), 1913
Oil on canvas, 131.1 x 200 cm. Solomon R. Guggenheim Museum, New York
Solomon R. Guggenheim Founding Collection 46.1040

FRANZ MARC *Dreaming Horse* (*Träumendes Pferd*), 1913

Watercolor, gouache, ink, and graphite on paper, 39.6 x 46.8 cm

Solomon R. Guggenheim Museum, New York

Solomon R. Guggenheim Founding Collection 44.937

FRANZ MARC *Stables (Stallungen)*, 1913

Oil on canvas, 73.6 x 157.5 cm. Solomon R. Guggenheim Museum, New York

Solomon R. Guggenheim Founding Collection 46.1037

PAUL KLEE *Flower Bed* (*Blumenbeet*), 1913

Oil on cardboard, 28.2 x 33.7 cm. Solomon R. Guggenheim Museum, New York

Estate of Karl Nierendorf, By purchase 48.1172.109

OTTO GUTFREUND *Embracing Figures* (*Objímající se postavy*), 1913

Plaster with blue patina, 65.1 x 32 x 23.8 cm. Solomon R. Guggenheim Museum, New York 87.3511

ANDRÉ DERAIN *Portrait of a Young Man* (*Portrait de jeune homme*), ca. 1913–14

Oil on canvas with graphite underdrawing, 91.8 x 73.6 cm

Solomon R. Guggenheim Museum, New York 59.1548

JEAN METZINGER *Landscape*, ca. 1913–14

Oil on canvas, 91.7 x 73 cm. Solomon R. Guggenheim Museum, New York

Solomon R. Guggenheim Founding Collection 40.841

JUAN GRIS *Violin Hanging on a Wall* (*Le violon accroché*), 1913

Crayon and india ink on paper, 70.2 x 44.1 cm. Solomon R. Guggenheim Museum, New York

Gift, Fuller Foundation, Inc. 84.3156

PABLO PICASSO *Woman with Guitar* (*Femme à la guitare*), winter 1913–14

Graphite on paper, 63 x 47.5 cm. Solomon R. Guggenheim Museum, New York 57.1488

MARC CHAGALL *The Flying Carriage* (*La calèche volante*), 1913

Oil on canvas, 106.7 x 120.1 cm. Solomon R. Guggenheim Museum, New York

Solomon R. Guggenheim Founding Collection 49.1212

MARC CHAGALL *Paris Through the Window* (*Paris par la fenêtre*), 1913

Oil on canvas, 135.8 x 141.4 cm. Solomon R. Guggenheim Museum, New York

Solomon R. Guggenheim Founding Collection, By gift 37.438

PIET MONDRIAN *Tableau No. 2/Composition No. VII*, 1913
Oil on canvas, 104.4 x 113.6 cm. Solomon R. Guggenheim Museum, New York
Solomon R. Guggenheim Founding Collection 49.1228. © 2011 Mondrian/Holtzman
Trust c/o HCR International Virginia

1913

FERNAND LÉGER Study for *Contrast of Forms* (Étude pour *Contraste de formes*), 1913

Oil on paper, mounted on board, 49.6 x 61.2 cm

Solomon R. Guggenheim Museum, New York

Estate of Karl Nierendorf, By purchase 48.1172.50

FERNAND LÉGER *Contrast of Forms* (*Contraste de formes*), 1913

Oil on burlap, 98.8 x 125 cm. Solomon R. Guggenheim Museum, New York

Solomon R. Guggenheim Founding Collection, By gift 38.345

GIACOMO BALLA *Paths of Movement + Dynamic Sequences*

(*Linee andamentali + successioni dinamiche*), 1913

Tempera on paper, mounted on canvas, 49 x 68 cm. Gianni Mattioli Collection, on long-term loan to the Peggy Guggenheim Collection, Venice

UMBERTO BOCCIONI *Dynamism of a Cyclist* (*Dinamismo di un ciclista*), 1913
Oil on canvas, 70 x 95 cm. Gianni Mattioli Collection, on long-term loan
to the Peggy Guggenheim Collection, Venice

UMBERTO BOCCIONI *Unique Forms of Continuity in Space* (*Forme uniche della continuità nello spazio*), 1913 (cast 2005)
Bronze, 112 x 90 x 40 cm. Private collection

NATALIA GONCHAROVA *Cats (rayist percep.[tion] in rose, black, and yellow)*
(*Koshki [luchistoe vospr.(iiatie) rozovoe, chernoe i zheltoe]*), 1913
Oil on canvas, 84.4 x 83.8 cm. Solomon R. Guggenheim Museum, New York 57.1484

ALEXANDER ARCHIPENKO *Boxing* (*The Struggle*) (*La Lutte*), 1913–14

Painted plaster, 60.3 x 42.2 x 40.6 cm

Solomon R. Guggenheim Museum, New York 55.1436

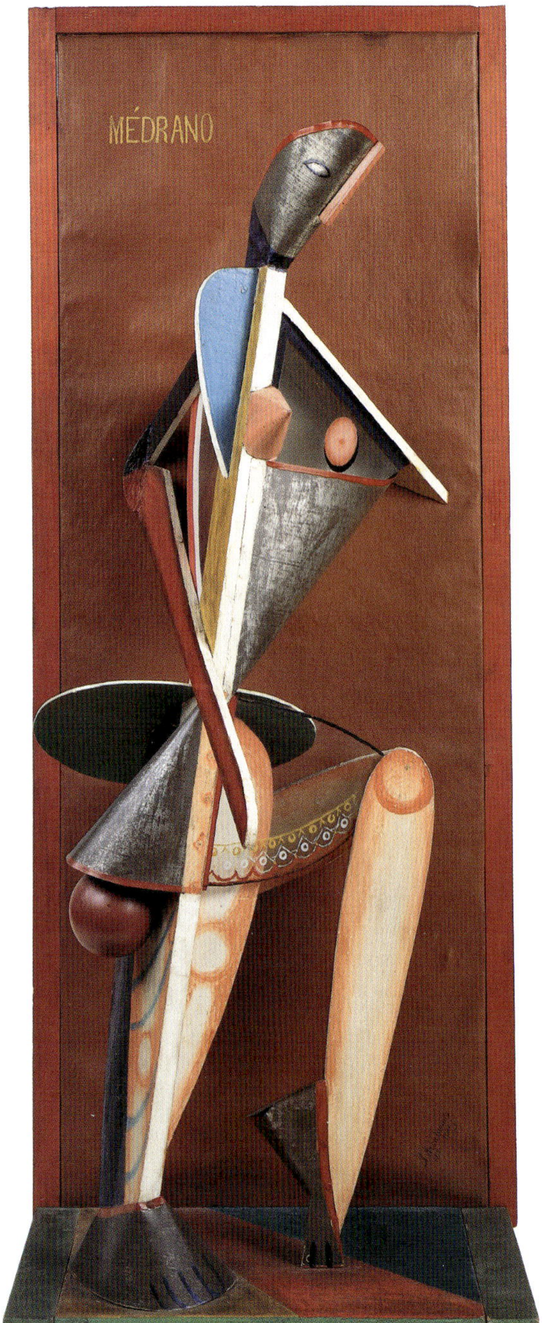

ALEXANDER ARCHIPENKO *Médrano II*, 1913–14

Painted tin, wood, glass, and painted oilcloth, 126.6 x 51.5 x 31.7 cm

Solomon R. Guggenheim Museum, New York 56.1445

ALEXANDER ARCHIPENKO *Carrousel Pierrot*, 1913

Painted plaster, 61 x 48.6 x 34 cm. Solomon R. Guggenheim Museum, New York 57.1483

VASILY KANDINSKY *Painting with White Border* (*Bild mit weissem Rand*), May 1913

Oil on canvas, 140.3 x 200.3 cm. Solomon R. Guggenheim Museum, New York

Solomon R. Guggenheim Founding Collection, By gift 37.245

VASILY KANDINSKY *Black Lines* (*Schwarze Linien*), December 1913
Oil on canvas, 129.4 x 131.1 cm. Solomon R. Guggenheim Museum, New York
Solomon R. Guggenheim Founding Collection, By gift 37.241

VASILY KANDINSKY *Light Picture* (*Helles Bild*), December 1913

Oil and natural resin on canvas, 77.8 x 100.2 cm. Solomon R. Guggenheim Museum, New York

Solomon R. Guggenheim Founding Collection, By gift 37.244

1914–18

JANUARY Der Sturm gallery, Berlin, hosts the final exhibition of Der Blaue Reiter (The Blue Rider).

FEBRUARY Charlie Chaplin's debut film, *Making a Living*, premieres in the United States. • Last exhibition of the Skupina výtvarných umělců (Group of Plastic Artists) opens in Prague's town hall. • Filippo Tommaso Marinetti's *Zang Tumb Tumb. Adrianopoli, Ottobre 1912* (Zang Tumb Tumb. Adrianople, October 1912), a collection of poems written in the words-in-freedom style that he formulated, is published.

MARCH Giovanni Giolitti resigns from his position as prime minister of Italy. • Wyndham Lewis forms the Rebel Art Centre in London.

APRIL First concert of **Luigi Russolo**'s music for eighteen *intonarumori* is held in Milan. • **Paul Klee**, August Macke, and Louis Moilliet spend two weeks in Tunisia. • Rome's Sprovieri gallery mounts an international Futurist exhibition.

MAY **Natalia Goncharova** travels to Paris with **Mikhail Larionov** and designs the set for the ballet *Le coq d'or* (*The Golden Cockerel*). • Vladimir Tatlin exhibits his first abstract painterly reliefs of metal, glass, and wood in his Moscow studio.

JUNE Archduke Franz Ferdinand, heir to the Austrian throne, is assassinated in Sarajevo on June 28. • Der Sturm presents **Marc Chagall**'s first solo exhibition. • **Fernand Léger**'s "Les réalisations picturales actuelles" ("Contemporary Achievements in Painting") is published in Guillaume Apollinaire's magazine *Les Soirées de Paris* (1912–14). • James Joyce's *Dubliners* is published in London.

JULY Vorticism officially begins in London with the publication of the manifesto *Blast* in the first of only two issues of the eponymous periodical (1914–15).

AUGUST World War I begins on August 1 with Germany's declaration of war on Russia. • **Alexei Jawlensky**, **Vasily Kandinsky**, and Marianne von Werefkin leave Munich for Switzerland. **Chagall** and **Piet Mondrian**, each visiting his native country, are prevented from returning to Paris. Macke and **Franz Marc** volunteer for the German army. **Larionov** is conscripted into the Russian army. Apollinaire, **Georges Braque**, **André Derain**, **Raymond Duchamp-Villon**, **Albert Gleizes**, and **Léger** are among those mobilized for the French army. **Oskar Kokoschka** soon joins the Austro-Hungarian cavalry.

Names in bold refer to artists in the exhibition.

SEPTEMBER **Umberto Boccioni**, **Carlo Carrà**, Marinetti, Ugo Piatti, and **Russolo** sign the "Sintesi futurista della guerra" ("Futurist Synthesis of the War") in Milan. • Futurists stage demonstrations in support of Italian intervention in Austria-Hungary. • In autumn, the French government sequesters the art collections of German-Jewish dealers Daniel-Henry Kahnweiler and Wilhelm Uhde as property of the German enemy; both collections are sold in postwar auctions.

1915

JANUARY First transcontinental telephone connection is made between Alexander Graham Bell in New York and Thomas Watson in San Francisco.

FEBRUARY **Marc** finishes writing his "100 Aphorismen" ("100 Aphorisms") from the front.

MARCH **Kazimir Malevich** and Tatlin participate in *Tramvai V: Pervaya futuristicheskaya vystavka kartin* (*Tramway V: The First Futurist Exhibition of Paintings*) at the Association for the Promotion of the Arts in Petrograd. • **Giacomo Balla** and Fortunato Depero's *Ricostruzione futurista dell'universo* (*Futurist Reconstruction of the Universe*) is published.

APRIL German troops first use poison gas on April 22 at the Second Battle of Ypres in Belgium.

MAY A German U-boat torpedoes the *RMS Lusitania* on May 7, precipitating U.S. entry into the war. • Italy enters the war on the Allied side on May 23. • **Boccioni**, Marinetti, **Russolo**, and **Mario Sironi** join the Battaglione Lombardo Volontari Ciclisti (Lombard Volunteer Cyclists Battalion). • **Giorgio de Chirico** leaves France for Italy, where he is conscripted into the army.

JUNE Vorticists exhibit at the Doré galleries in London. • **Goncharova** and **Larionov** leave Russia for Switzerland. • **Egon Schiele** is conscripted into the Austro-Hungarian army.

NOVEMER Franz Kafka's novella *Die Verwandlung* (*The Metamorphosis*) is published in Leipzig, Germany.

DECEMBER **Malevich** exhibits his Suprematist paintings at *Posledniaia futuris-ticheskaya vystavka kartin, "0.10"* (*nul-desat*) (*The Last Futurist Exhibition of Paintings, "0.10"* [*Zero-Ten*]) at the Galerie Dobychina in Petrograd. • **Malevich**'s manifesto "Ot kubizma k suprematizmu. Novyi zhivopisnyi realizm" ("From Cubism to Suprematism: The New Painterly Realism") is published in Petrograd. • **Larionov** designs costumes and sets for the ballet *Soleil de nuit* (*Sun of the Night*), which travels from Geneva to Paris.

Pages 158–59: Franz Marc (third row, center) with his German battalion, France, 1915

1916

FEBRUARY Jean Arp and Tristan Tzara establish the Dada movement in Zurich, with Cabaret Voltaire as its headquarters. • Battle of Verdun, one of the war's most devastating and longest battles, begins on February 21.

MARCH Albert Einstein's "Hamiltonsches Prinzip und allgemeine Relativitätstheorie" ("Hamilton's Principle and the General Theory of Relativity") is published in Berlin. • **Marc** dies on the Western Front. • In an empty shop at 17 Petrovka Street in Moscow, Tatlin organizes the Futurist exhibition *Magazin* (*The Store*), which showcases among others, the work of **Malevich**, **Liubov Popova**, and Alexander Rodchenko.

JULY Battle of the Somme begins on July 1; the British army soon introduces the use of tanks in modern warfare on this battlefield.

AUGUST **Boccioni** dies from a fall from his horse during military exercises.

SEPTEMBER Munich Secession and Der Sturm (in November) organize commemorative exhibitions of **Marc**'s work.

DECEMBER **Balla** designs the set for Igor Stravinsky's *Feu d'artifice* (*Fireworks*).
• Amédée Ozenfant's "Notes sur le cubisme" ("Notes on Cubism") is published in *L'elan*.
• Karl I succeeds Franz Josef as emperor of Austria-Hungary.

1917

FEBRUARY Revolution overthrows the imperial government in Petrograd, forcing Czar Nicholas II to abdicate on March 15 (March 2 in the Julian calendar).

APRIL United States officially enters World War I on April 6. • In Petrograd, Vladimir Lenin issues his "Aprel'skie tezisy" ("April Theses"), promoting the establishment of a workers' state.

MAY Apollinaire coins the term "Surrealism" in the program for Jean Cocteau and Erik Satie's ballet *Parade*, which premieres in Paris.

JUNE **Ernst Ludwig Kirchner** moves to Frauenkirch, Switzerland, after the trauma of wartime service relegates him to various stints in sanatoria.

OCTOBER **Mondrian** and Theo van Doesburg begin publication of *De Stijl* (1917–32) in Leiden, Netherlands.

NOVEMBER Bolsheviks and Left Socialist Revolutionaries stage a coup in Petrograd on November 7 (October 25 in the Julian calendar), which leads to the formation of a new Bolshevik government.

1917–18

DECEMBER British forces occupy Jerusalem on December 9. • This year the Constructivist group forms, and **Carrà** and **de Chirico** found the group later known as Scuola Metafisica (School of Metaphysical Painting).

1918

JANUARY Richard Huelsenbeck founds the Berlin Dada movement.

FEBRUARY Women's suffrage is achieved in Great Britain on February 6. • Worldwide influenza epidemic kills Gustav Klimt. **Schiele** and Apollinaire are killed as a result of the virus later in the year. • Joan Miró's first solo exhibition opens at the Galeries Dalmau in Barcelona; this year the Agrupació Courbet (Courbet Group) forms around the artist.

MARCH Russia's capital moves from Petrograd to Moscow on March 12. • With the Treaty of Brest-Litovsk signed on March 3, Finland, Latvia, Lithuania, and Ukraine become independent from Russia.

JULY Bolsheviks execute Nicholas II and his family during the night of July 16–17 in the Siberian city of Yekaterinburg. • Tzara writes the seminal "Manifest Dada" ("Dada Manifesto") in Zurich. • *Gestalt und Wirklichkeit,* the first of Oswald Spengler's two volume *Der Untergang des Abendlandes* (*The Decline of the West*) is published in Munich.

AUGUST **Chagall** is appointed Commissar for Art in the province of Vitebsk.

OCTOBER **Kandinsky** leads Svobodnye gosudarstvennye khudozhestvennye masterskie (SVOMAS) (Free State Art Schools), a painting studio in Moscow. • Sergei Shchukin's collection of French art and the building that houses it are nationalized in Russia; Ivan Morozov's art collection is nationalized in December.

NOVEMBER Kaiser Wilhelm II of Germany abdicates on November 9 and flees to Holland; the Weimar Republic is founded. • Armistice ends World War I on November 11. • Austro-Hungarian Empire dissolves when Kaiser Karl I effectively abdicates on November 12 and goes into exile. Czechoslovakia, Hungary, Poland, and Serbia become sovereign states. • **Mondrian**, Van Doesburg, and others sign the "Manifest I of 'De Stijl,'" published in *De Stijl*. • *Après le cubisme* (*After Cubism*), the manifesto of Purism by Ozenfant and Charles-Édouard Jeanneret (Le Corbusier), is published in Paris in conjunction with the first Purist exhibition. • Max Pechstein and Cesar Klein initiate the Novembergruppe (November Group) union of artists, architects, and writers in Berlin. • Bruno Taut establishes the Arbeitsrat für Kunst (Workers' Council for Art). Members include **Lyonel Feininger**, Walter Gropius, and Ludwig Meidner.

THE FALLEN BLUE RIDER: FRANZ MARC AND THE GREAT WAR

MEGAN M. FONTANELLA

> The Blue Rider has fallen, a mighty, biblical figure about whom there hung a fragrance of Eden. Across the landscape he cast a blue shadow. He was the one who could still hear the animals speak; and he transfigured their uncomprehended souls.
>
> ELSE LASKER-SCHÜLER, 1916[1]

Germany's declaration of war on Russia on August 1, 1914, marked the abrupt end to a flourishing artistic era that had only just begun. The widespread transnational exhibitions of the early 1910s virtually ceased and several of the most innovative modernist groups in Europe disbanded as their members parted ways, joined the war effort, or were suddenly recast as enemy aliens. Vasily Kandinsky, who had lived in Germany for sixteen years, was forced to leave due to his Russian citizenship. The artist described the devastating displacement in a letter to his Berlin gallerist Herwarth Walden: "I feel as if torn from a dream. . . . I was living in a time when such things would be impossible. My illusion was taken from me. Mountains of corpses, all kinds of dreadful torments, spiritual culture wound back for an indefinite time."[2] French artist Albert Gleizes echoed Kandinsky's fatalism: "The present conflict throws into anarchy all of the intellectual paths of the prewar period, and the reasons are simple: the leaders are in the army and the generation of thirty-year-olds is sparse. . . . The past is finished."[3]

One artist was instead swept up in a collective surge of patriotism in the summer of 1914. Franz Marc, along with August Macke, was among the first volunteers for active service in the German army. Within weeks at the barracks in Munich, he was promoted from corporal to noncommissioned officer, and later, to lieutenant (fig. 18). His unit was moved to the western front at the end of August. Though discouraged by the interruption to his painting, throughout his service Marc made drawings and wrote many letters to his wife, Maria, as well as colleagues and friends. These wartime letters not only document his unbroken search to define his identity as an artist, but also reveal his conflicted state of mind regarding the cataclysmic events he witnessed as an infantryman, and offer a glimpse at what might have transpired had he survived.[4]

Marc's motives for enlisting were largely a reflection of the spiritual ideals he had explored earlier in the decade as a member of Der Blaue Reiter (The Blue Rider), the Munich-based Expressionist group he cofounded with Kandinsky in 1911. The group believed that the material and spiritual forces of the world were increasingly at odds with one another. The war, however, held the promise of restoring religiosity through a radical cleansing of the impurities pervading Europe. Marc's conviction was less about war fervor, but rather, as he conveyed to Kandinsky, that there was simply "no other way to the era of the spirit."[5] Marc was certainly not the only artist to exalt the abstract concept of war or appropriate the vocabulary of conflict. In the first Futurist manifesto, published in 1909, Filippo Tommaso Marinetti declared: "We intend to glorify war—the only hygiene of the world—militarism, patriotism, the destructive gesture of anarchists."[6] In his 1912 essay "Die 'Wilden' Deutschlands" ("The 'Savages' of Germany"), Marc similarly characterized the avant-garde plight as a "battle" that, revealing his romantic outlook, "seems to be unequal, but spiritual matters are never decided by numbers, only by the power of ideas."[7]

Marc employed war imagery and apocalyptic themes in his prewar painting too, in order to symbolize the quest for spiritual redemption. Still, the prescience of this body of work was disarming after he became a direct participant in the European conflict. In March 1915, Marc's patron and friend Bernhard Koehler sent the infantryman a Der Sturm gallery postcard featuring a reproduction of his *Fate of the Animals (The Trees Show their Rings, the Animals their Veins)* (*Tierschicksale [Die Bäume zeigten ihre Ringe, die Tiere ihre Adern],* 1913, fig. 19). The painting is one of a series of works, including *The Unfortunate Land of Tyrol* (*Das arme Land Tyrol*, 1913, p. 131), executed during Marc's last full year of work that responds to the skirmishes, war preparations, and overall mounting political tensions of 1911–14 (what Marc called the "latent war" in peace).[8] He described to Maria the poignant effect of revisiting *Fate of the Animals* while in the midst of combat: "It is like a premonition of the war, horrifying and moving; I can hardly imagine that I painted it. . . . There is an artistic logic in having painted such works *before* the war, rather than their being stupid reminiscences *after* the war. At that point one will have to paint *constructive*, future paintings, not memories."[9]

As the war unfolded, Marc's early enthusiasm increasingly gave way to disillusionment and concern regarding the rise in extreme nationalism. Marc, on the other hand, promoted a spirit

Fig. 18 Franz Marc on leave from the German army, with Maria Marc, July 1915

of collaboration and exchange that defined modernist culture in the prewar years. His cosmopolitanism was consistent with the attitude of the Blaue Reiter, whose internationally oriented outlook was perhaps most clearly voiced in Kandinsky and Marc's unpublished preface to *Der Blaue Reiter* (*The Blaue Reiter Almanac*, 1912): "As with a personality, the national element is automatically reflected in each great work. But in the last resort this national coloration is merely incidental. The whole work, called art, knows no borders or nations, only humanity."[10] Marc further proclaimed the commonality of the avant-garde in the almanac's subscription prospectus: "There is an artistic tension all over Europe. Everywhere new artists are greeting each other; a look, a handshake is enough for them to understand each other!"[11]

Marc's friendship with the French artist Robert Delaunay, who participated in the Blaue Reiter exhibitions in 1911 and 1912, was just one manifestation of his belief in the transnational unanimity of modernism. After a visit to Delaunay's studio in Paris in autumn 1912, his series of *Windows* (*Fenêtres*, 1912–14, p. 112) left a strong impression on Marc as evidenced in *Stables* (*Stallungen*, 1913, p. 133), where his favorite subject—the horse—is almost indistinguishable within the structure of parallel and crossing diagonals. The artists met again a year later at the Erster deutscher Herbstsalon (First German Autumn Salon), one of the last great exhibitions in Germany of vanguard art before the war (fig. 20). On this occasion it was Delaunay's latest and completely abstract *Circular Forms* (*Formes circulaires*) paintings that influenced Marc's final pictures from 1914, including *Broken Forms* (*Zerbrochene Formen*, p. 171).[12]

Nevertheless, the mobilization order immediately strained Marc's relationships with his contemporaries. He agonized over the fate of the artistic community and his spiritual kinship with Kandinsky, in particular: "I have the sorrowful feeling that this war will flow between us and divide us like a great torrent; the one can barely see the other on the distant bank. . . . At such a time everyone, whether he will or no, is snatched back into his [own] nation."[13]

Fig. 19 Franz Marc, *Fate of the Animals (The Trees Show their Rings, the Animals their Veins)* (*Tierschicksale [Die Bäume zeigten ihre Ringe, die Tiere ihre Adern]*), 1913. Oil on canvas, 195 x 263.5 cm. Kunstmuseum Basel

Fig. 20 Postcard sent by Robert Delaunay in Paris to Franz Marc in Sindelsdorf, Germany, August 8, 1913. The card bears a stamp from the Erster deutscher Herbstsalon (First German Autumn Salon)

Despite asserting his own stance as a European first and a German second, Marc observed a widespread xenophobia affecting the nation. His first essay written from the front, "Im Fegefeuer des Krieges" ("In War's Purifying Fire"), was published in December 1914 in *Vossische Zeitung*, a national newspaper with one of the largest readerships in Germany. The artist voiced his argument for the necessary "blood sacrifice" of war and his hope for a new world order, but also cautioned against "narrow-hearted nationalism" should Germany prove victorious at the war's end: "We are rich and strong enough to dispense with forts in time of war so we can do without fences in peace time."[14] Most of all, the war brought not the purifying purge that Marc had naïvely envisioned, but unspeakable trauma and devastation. The news of Macke's death in battle in September 1914 dealt an early blow to Marc's confidence in the journey they had enthusiastically started together just two months prior. In an obituary, Marc wrote that his friend's life represented "one of the boldest and most beautiful curves in the development of German art," and with his death that curve was rudely broken.[15]

By the time he received a ten-day home leave from the front in July 1915, Marc's conflicted mental state was palpable. Paul Klee observed in his diary that "the continuous pressure and loss of freedom clearly weighed on him. . . . He ought to hate the soldier's game more than he does, or even better, it ought to be indifferent to him."[16] Yet in his letters to his wife Marc revealed his private doubts in a war that had "lasted too long and become meaningless."[17] At the start of 1916, he lamented the incessant bloodshed of the previous year: "It is horrible to think of it—and all of this for *nothing*. . . . One has to relearn and rethink everything to absorb this uncanny *psychology of action*, not to hate it, to insult it, to mock it, or to mourn it, but to understand its origin and—to create *counter ideas*."[18] The escalating casualties were equally distressing to the officials in Berlin. By February 1916, the decision was made to withdraw from combat a number of "outstandingly talented individuals." Tragically, Marc would be killed before the directive could be carried out.[19]

In spite of his continued frustration, depression, and solitude as an infantryman, Marc's final words to Maria on March 4, 1916, were hopeful: "Yes, this year I will come back to my undestroyed dear house, to you and my work. Amidst the limitless awful pictures of destruction in which I am now living, this thought of returning home has a halo, which cannot be described sufficiently with lovely words."[20] The artist was fatally wounded that afternoon; while on a

Fig. 21 Franz Marc on the French front. This photograph was included in the last letter Marc sent to the gallerist Herwarth Walden in Berlin, March 1, 1916

reconnaissance mission in the French town of Braquis, shell splinters struck his temple. Walden, who assembled a memorial exhibition at his gallery that November, published in the periodical *Der Sturm*: "Now an artist has fallen who cannot die" (fig. 21).[21]

Many historians have considered the magnitude of what was lost with the death of Franz Marc, as with so many other visionaries who did not survive the Great War. The world to which Marc would have returned in 1918 was vastly different from the one he left in 1914, which had been brimming with creativity and energy. Klee also suggested that Marc's service on the western front might make him "a completely different man someday."[22] Regardless of whether he would have again formed a confederation of artists or determined to "'form' things alone," returned to the animal subjects he held dear or completely reinvented his artistic style, Marc's outlook from the front was simple: "My main thought now is: the concept of a new world; always to create, to work *for the future*."[23]

Notes

1 Else Lasker-Schüler, *Berliner Tageblatt*, March 9, 1916, quoted in Peter-Klaus Schuster, *Franz Marc: Postcards to Prince Jussuf* (Munich: Prestel-Verlag, 1988), p. 25. An Expressionist artist, poet, and writer, and the first wife of avant-garde promoter Herwarth Walden, Lasker-Schüler began corresponding with Franz Marc in autumn 1912 and the two forged a close artistic friendship.

2 Vasily Kandinsky to Herwarth Walden, August 2, 1914, quoted in Robin Lenman, *Artists and Society in Germany, 1850–1914* (Manchester: Manchester University Press, 1997), p. 185. Kandinsky left Germany for Switzerland on August 3, 1914, and eventually returned to his native Russia.

3 Albert Gleizes, *Le mot*, May 1, 1915, quoted in Milton A. Cohen, *Movement, Manifesto, Melee: The Modernist Group 1910–1914* (Lanham, Md.: Lexington Books, 2004), p. 176.

4 Marc's last artistic work was the *Sketchbook from the Field* (*Skizzenbuch aus dem Felde*, 1915), a collection of thirty-six pencil and pen-and-ink drawings. His wartime letters to his wife Maria, letters to August Macke's widow Elizabeth, the famous "100 Aphorismen" ("100 Aphorisms," 1914–15), and additional documents were published posthumously in Franz Marc, *Briefe, Aufzeichnungen und Aphorismen* (Berlin: Paul Cassirer, 1920).

5 Franz Marc to Vasily Kandinsky, September 26, 1914, quoted in Lenman, *Artists and Society in Germany*, p. 185.

6 Filippo Tommaso Marinetti, "Manifeste du futurisme" ("Manifesto of Futurism"), *Le Figaro*, February 20, 1909, reprinted as "The Founding and Manifesto of Futurism," Lawrence Rainey, Christine Poggi, and Laura Wittman, eds., *Futurism: An Anthology* (New Haven, Conn.: Yale University Press, 2009), p. 51.

7 Franz Marc, "Die 'Wilden' Deutschlands" ("The 'Savages' of Germany"), *Der Blaue Reiter*, ed. Vasily Kandinsky and Franz Marc (Munich: R. Piper & Co. Verlag, 1912), reprinted in *The Blaue Reiter Almanac*, new documentary edition, ed. Klaus Lankheit, trans. Henning Falkenstein (Boston: MFA Publications, 2005), pp. 61–64.

8 Franz Marc to Maria Marc, June 21, 1915, reprinted in Franz Marc, *Letters from the War*, ed. Klaus Lankheit and Uwe Steffan, trans. Liselotte Dieckmann (New York: Peter Lang Publishing, 1992), p. 57.

9 Franz Marc to Maria Marc, March 17, 1915, ibid., p. 34 (Marc's emphasis).

10 Typescript preface by Vasily Kandinsky and Franz Marc from August Macke's estate, October 1911, reprinted in *The Blaue Reiter Almanac*, pp. 250–51.

11 Franz Marc, "Der Blaue Reiter," text of the subscription prospectus, mid-January 1912, ibid., p. 252.

12 For a thorough discussion of the relationship between Robert Delaunay, August Macke, and Franz Marc see *Marc, Macke, und Delaunay. Die Schönheit einer zerbrechenden Welt (1910–1914)*, exh. cat. (Hannover: DuMont, 2009).

13 Franz Marc to Vasily Kandinsky, October 24, 1914, quoted in Lenman, *Artists and Society in Germany*, p. 185.

14 Franz Marc, "Im Fegefeuer des Krieges," *Vossische Zeitung*, no. 637, December 15, 1914, p. 2f. Reprinted in Victor H. Miesel, ed., *Voices of German Expressionism* (Englewood Cliffs, N.J.: Prentice-Hall, Inc., 1970), pp. 160–64.

15 Franz Marc, Hageville, France, October 25, 1914, published in Marc, *Briefe, Aufzeichnungen und Aphorismen*, p. 143. Reprinted in *Franz Marc Schriften*, ed. Klaus Lankheit (Cologne: DuMont Buchverlag, 1978), pp. 156–57. Reflecting on Macke's death by "enemy bullet," Marc noted: "one could almost say a friendly one, for it was French." Franz Marc to Maria Marc, February 22, 1916, reprinted in Marc, *Letters from the War*, p. 109.

16 Paul Klee, *The Diaries of Paul Klee, 1898–1918*, ed. Felix Klee (Berkeley: University of California Press, 1992), pp. 319–23.

17 Franz Marc to Maria Marc, July 1, 1915, quoted in Ida Katherine Rigby, "Franz Marc's Wartime Letters from the Front," *Franz Marc: 1880–1916*, exh. cat. (Berkeley: University of California, 1979), p. 62.

18 Franz Marc to Maria Marc, New Year, 1916, reprinted in Marc, *Letters from the War*, p. 95 (Marc's emphasis).

19 Richard Seewald to Maria Marc, February 4, 1916, quoted in Rosel Gollek, *Franz Marc, 1880–1916*, exh. cat. (Munich: Prestel-Verlag, 1980), p. 47.

20 Franz Marc to Maria Marc, March 4, 1916, reprinted in Marc, *Letters from the War*, p. 113 (Marc's emphasis).

21 Herwarth Walden, *Der Sturm* 6, no. 23–24 (1916), quoted in Sigrid Bauschinger, "The Berlin Moderns: Else Lasker-Schüler and Café Culture," *Berlin Metropolis: Jews and the New Culture, 1890–1918*, ed. Emily D. Bilski, exh. cat. (Berkeley: University of California Press, 1999), p. 81.

22 Klee continues: "I often anxiously surmised that he would return to earthly simplicity, once the ferment was over, that he would not come back in order to rouse the world to some grand vision, but entirely from a human impulse." Klee, *The Diaries of Paul Klee*, p. 344.

23 Franz Marc to Maria Marc, March 14, 1915, and March 27, 1915, reprinted in Marc, *Letters from the War*, pp. 34–35 (Marc's emphasis).

FRANZ MARC *Broken Forms* (*Zerbrochene Formen*), 1914

Oil on canvas, 111.8 x 84.4 cm. Solomon R. Guggenheim Museum, New York 50.1240

ENRICO PRAMPOLINI *Simultaneous Self-Portrait* (*Autoritratto simultaneo*), 1914

Oil on canvas, 100.6 x 100.6 cm. Solomon R. Guggenheim Museum, New York

Solomon R. Guggenheim Founding Collection 46.1020

ALBERT GLEIZES *Portrait of an Army Doctor* (*Portrait d'un médecin militaire*), 1914–15
Oil on canvas, 119.8 x 95.1 cm. Solomon R. Guggenheim Museum, New York
Solomon R. Guggenheim Founding Collection, By gift 37.473

CONSTANTIN BRANCUSI *Little French Girl* (*The First Step [III]*) (*La jeune fille française*), ca. 1914–18
Oak, 123.5 x 23.8 x 23.5 cm; base: 27.9 x 33 x 37.1 cm. Solomon R. Guggenheim Museum, New York
Gift, Estate of Katherine S. Dreier 53.1332

PIET MONDRIAN *Composition 8* (*Compositie 8*), 1914

Oil on canvas, 94.4 x 55.6 cm. Solomon R. Guggenheim Museum, New York

Solomon R. Guggenheim Founding Collection 49.1227. © 2011 Mondrian/Holtzman Trust

c/o HCR International Virginia

PIET MONDRIAN *Composition* (*Compositie*), 1916

Oil on canvas, with wood, 119 x 75.1 cm. Solomon R. Guggenheim Museum, New York

Solomon R. Guggenheim Founding Collection 49.1229. © 2011 Mondrian/Holtzman Trust c/o HCR International Virginia

JUAN GRIS *Cherries (Les cerises)*, 1915

Oil on canvas, 54.6 x 38.1 cm. Solomon R. Guggenheim Museum, New York

Bequest, Richard S. Zeisler 2007.42

JUAN GRIS *Newspaper and Fruit Dish* (*Journal et compotier*), March 1916
Oil on canvas, 46 x 37.8 cm. Solomon R. Guggenheim Museum, New York
Gift, Estate of Katherine S. Dreier 53.1341

GINO SEVERINI *Red Cross Train Passing a Village* (*Train de la Croix Rouge traversant un village*), summer 1915
Oil on canvas, 88.9 x 116.2 cm. Solomon R. Guggenheim Museum, New York
Solomon R. Guggenheim Founding Collection 44.944

LYONEL FEININGER *Gelmeroda IV*, 1915

Oil on canvas, 100 x 79.7 cm. Solomon R. Guggenheim Museum, New York 54.1410

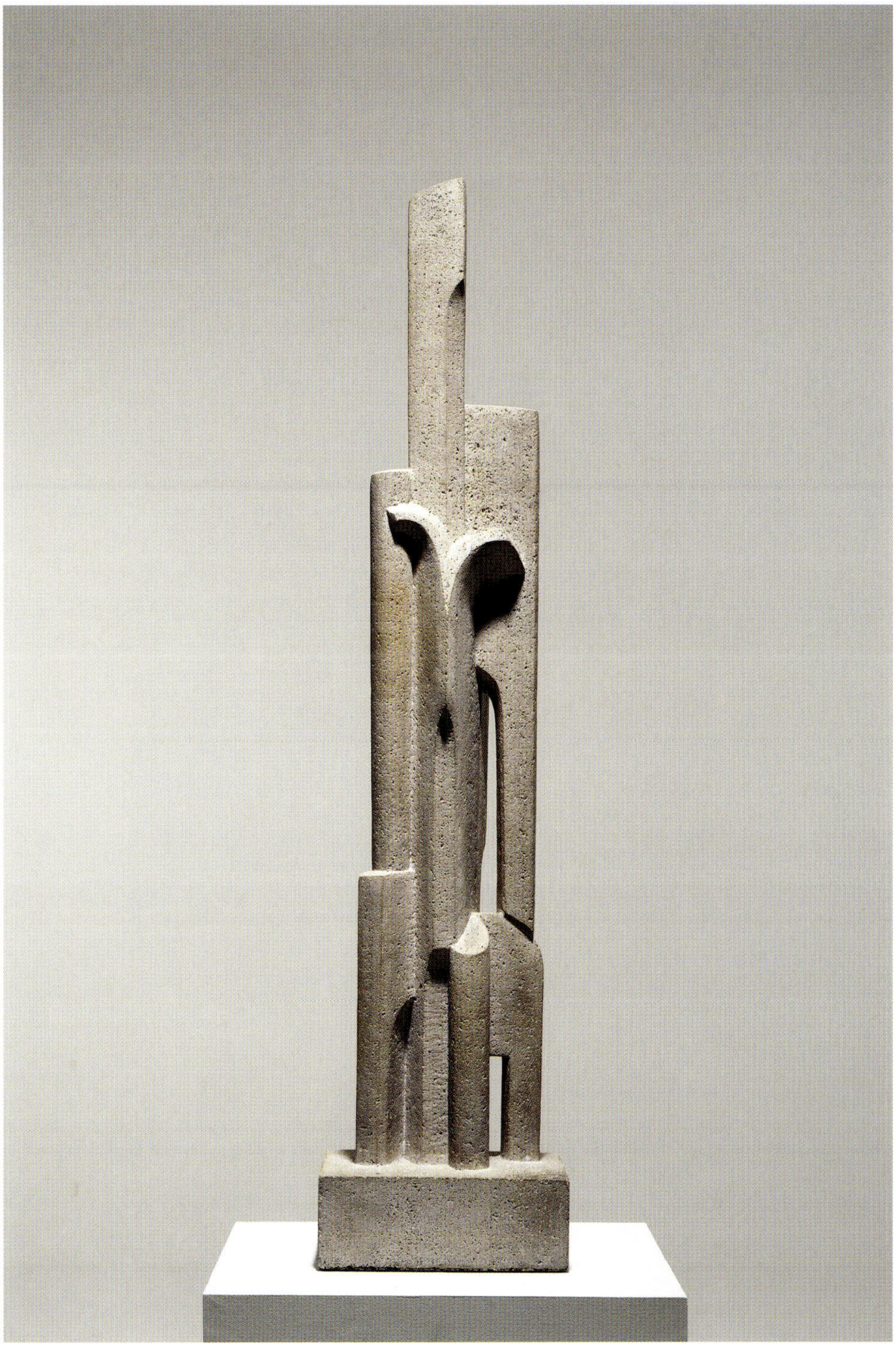

JACQUES LIPCHITZ *Standing Personage* (*Personage debout*), 1916

Limestone, 106.7 x 26 x 20.3 cm. Solomon R. Guggenheim Museum, New York 58.1526

OSKAR KOKOSCHKA *Knight Errant* (*Der irrende Ritter*), 1915
Oil on canvas, 89.5 x 180 cm. Solomon R. Guggenheim Museum, New York
Estate of Karl Nierendorf, By purchase 48.1172.380

ERNST LUDWIG KIRCHNER *Artillerymen (Das Soldatenbad)*, 1915

Oil on canvas, 140 x 153 cm. Solomon R. Guggenheim Museum, New York, By exchange 88.3591

EMIL NOLDE *Young Horses* (*Junge Pferde*), 1916

Oil on canvas, 72.4 x 100.3 cm. Solomon R. Guggenheim Museum, New York

Purchase and by exchange 79.2551

EGON SCHIELE *Portrait of Johann Harms* (*Porträt J. H.*), 1916

Oil with wax on canvas, 141 x 110.8 cm. Solomon R. Guggenheim Museum, New York

Partial gift, Dr. and Mrs. Otto Kallir 69.1884

GIACOMO BALLA *Spring* (*La primavera*), ca. 1916

Oil on canvas, 81.3 x 66.8 cm. Solomon R. Guggenheim Museum, New York, By exchange 88.3570.R

LIUBOV POPOVA *Birsk*, 1916

Oil on canvas, 106 x 69.5 cm. Solomon R. Guggenheim Museum, New York, Gift, George Costakis 81.2822.R

KAZIMIR MALEVICH *Untitled*, ca. 1916

Oil on canvas, 53 x 53 cm. The Solomon R. Guggenheim Foundation
Peggy Guggenheim Collection, Venice, Acquisition confirmed
in 2009 by agreement with the Heirs of Kazimir Malevich 76.2553.42

HENRI MATISSE *The Italian Woman* (*L'Italienne*), 1916

Oil on canvas, 116.7 x 89.5 cm. Solomon R. Guggenheim Museum, New York, By exchange 82.2946

AMEDEO MODIGLIANI *Nude* (*Nu*), 1917

Oil on canvas, 73 x 116.7 cm. Solomon R. Guggenheim Museum, New York

Solomon R. Guggenheim Founding Collection, By gift 41.535

MARIO SIRONI *War* (*La guerra*), 1919

Mixed media on paper, 77 x 61.8 cm. Private collection

KURT SCHWITTERS *Mountain Graveyard* (*Hochgebirgsfriedhof*), 1919

Oil on board, mounted on cork, 91.6 x 72.4 cm. Solomon R. Guggenheim Museum, New York

Gift, Mr. and Mrs. Frederick M. Stern 62.1617

ARTIST BIOGRAPHIES

ALEXANDER ARCHIPENKO

b. 1887, Kiev; d. 1964, New York

Alexander Archipenko was born on May 30, 1887, in Kiev. In 1902, he entered the Kiev Art School, where he studied painting and sculpture until 1905. During this time, he was impressed by the Byzantine icons, frescoes, and mosaics of Kiev. After a sojourn in Moscow, Archipenko moved to Paris in 1908. He attended the École des Beaux-Arts for a brief period and continued to study independently at the Musée du Louvre, where he was drawn to Egyptian, Assyrian, archaic Greek, and early Gothic sculpture. In 1910, he began exhibiting at the Salon des Indépendants in Paris, and the following year showed for the first time at the Salon d'Automne.

In 1912, Archipenko was given his first solo show in Germany at the Museum Folkwang, Hagen. That same year, in Paris, he opened the first of his many art schools; joined the Section d'Or (Golden Section) group, which included Georges Braque, Marcel Duchamp, Fernand Léger, and Pablo Picasso, among others; and produced his first painted reliefs, the *Sculpto-Peintures*. In 1913, Archipenko exhibited at the *International Exhibition of Modern Art* (popularly known as the Armory Show) in New York and made his first prints, which were reproduced in the Italian Futurist publication *Lacerba* (1913–15) in 1914. He participated in the Salon des Indépendants in 1914 and the Venice Biennale in 1920. During the war years, the artist resided in Cimiez, a suburb of Nice. From 1919 to 1921, he traveled to Geneva, Zurich, Paris, London, Brussels, Athens, and other European cities to exhibit his work. Archipenko's first solo show in the United States was held at the Société Anonyme, New York, in 1921.

In 1923, he moved to the United States, where over the years he opened art schools in New York City; Woodstock, New York; Los Angeles; and Chicago. In 1924, Archipenko invented his first kinetic work, *Archipentura*. For the next thirty years, he taught throughout the United States at art schools and universities, including the short-lived New Bauhaus. He became a U.S. citizen in 1928. Most of Archipenko's works in German museums were confiscated by the Nazis in their purge of *entartete kunst* (degenerate art). In 1947, he produced the first of his sculptures that are illuminated from within. He accompanied an exhibition of his work throughout Germany in 1955–56, and at this time began his book *Archipenko: Fifty Creative Years 1908–1958*, published in 1960. Archipenko died on February 25, 1964, in New York.

GIACOMO BALLA

b. 1871, Turin; d. 1958, Rome

Giacomo Balla was born in Turin on July 18, 1871. In 1891 he studied briefly at the Accademia Albertina di Belle Arti and the Liceo Artistico in Turin and exhibited for the first time under the aegis of the Società Promotrice di Belle Arti in that city. He studied at the University of Turin with Cesare Lombroso around 1892. In 1895 Balla moved to Rome, where he worked for several years as an illustrator, caricaturist, and portrait painter. In 1899 his work was included in the Venice Biennale and in the *Esposizione internazionale di belle arti* (*International Exhibition of Fine Arts*) at the galleries of the Società degli Amatori e Cultori di Belle Arti in Rome, where he exhibited regularly for the next ten years. In 1900, Balla spent seven months in Paris assisting the illustrator Serafino Macchiati. Around 1903 he began to instruct Umberto Boccioni and Gino Severini in Divisionist painting techniques. In that same year his work was exhibited at the *Esposizione internazionale d'arte della città di Venezia* (*International Art Exhibition of the City of Venice*) and in 1903 and 1904 at the Glaspalast in Munich. In 1904 Balla was represented in the *Internationale Kunstausstellung Düsseldorf* (*International Art Exhibition Düsseldorf*) and in 1909 exhibited at the Salon d'Automne in Paris.

Balla signed the second Futurist painting manifesto of 1910 with Boccioni, Carlo Carrà, Luigi Russolo, and Severini, although he did not exhibit with the group until 1913. In 1912 he traveled to London and to Düsseldorf, where he began painting his abstract light studies. In 1913 Balla participated in the Erster deutscher Herbstsalon (First German Autumn Salon) at

Herwarth Walden's Der Sturm gallery in Berlin and in an exhibition at the Rotterdamsche Kunstkring in Rotterdam. In 1914 he experimented with sculpture for the first time and showed it in the *Prima esposizione libera futurista* (*First Free Futurist Exhibition*) at the Galleria Sprovieri, Rome. He also designed and painted Futurist furniture and designed Futurist "anti-neutral" clothing. With Fortunato Depero, Balla wrote the manifesto *Ricostruzione futurista dell'universo* (*Futurist Reconstruction of the Universe*) in 1915. His first solo exhibitions were held that same year at the Società Italiana Lampade Elettriche "Z" and at the Sala d'arte A. Angelelli in Rome. His work was also shown in 1915 at the Panama-Pacific International Exposition in San Francisco. In 1918 he was given a solo show at the Casa d'arte Bragaglia in Rome. Balla continued to exhibit in Europe and the United States and in 1935 was made a member of the Accademia di San Luca in Rome. He died on March 1, 1958, in Rome.

UMBERTO BOCCIONI

b. 1882, Reggio Calabria, Italy; d. 1916, Sorte, Italy

Umberto Boccioni was born on October 19, 1882, in Reggio Calabria, Italy. In 1901 he went to Rome, where he studied design with a sign painter and attended the Scuola Libera del Nudo at the Accademia di Belle Arti. In Rome he and Gino Severini learned the techniques of Divisionist painting from Giacomo Balla. Boccioni traveled in 1902 to Paris, where he studied Impressionist and Post-Impressionist painting. He participated in the *Mostra dei rifiutati* in 1905 and in the *Esposizione di belle arti* (*Exhibition of Fine Arts*) in 1906, both in Rome.

Following a trip to Russia in 1906, Boccioni visited Padua and then moved to Venice, where he spent the winter of 1906–07 taking life-drawing classes at the Accademia di Belle Arti. In 1907 he settled in Milan. In 1909–10 Boccioni began to frequent the Famiglia Artistica (Artistic Family), a Milanese artists' society that sponsored annual exhibitions. During this period he associated with Carlo Carrà and Luigi Russolo, and met the poet Filippo Tommaso Marinetti, who had published the "Manifesto dei pittori futuristi" ("Manifesto of Futurist Painters") and the "Manifesto tecnico della pittura futurista" ("Technical Manifesto of Futurist Painting"). He, Carrà, Russolo, and Severini signed the first manifesto and were joined by Balla in signing the second. That same year Boccioni's first solo exhibition was held at the Galleria Ca' Pesaro in Venice.

In fall 1911 the artist went to Paris, where he met Pablo Picasso and Guillaume Apollinaire through Severini. Boccioni's paintings were shown with those of Carrà, Russolo, and Severini in the first Futurist exhibition in Paris, at the Bernheim-Jeune gallery in 1912. The exhibition then traveled to London, Berlin, Brussels, The Hague, Amsterdam, and Munich. In 1912 Boccioni began concentrating on sculpture, and his "Manifesto tecnico della scultura futurista" ("Technical Manifesto of Futurist Sculpture") was published. From 1912 to 1914 he contributed articles to the Futurist publication *Lacerba* (1913–15). In 1913 the artist showed sculpture and paintings in a solo show at the Galerie de la Boétie in Paris, and his sculpture was included in the inaugural exhibition of the Galleria Futurista Permanente in Rome. His book *Pittura e scultura futuriste* (*dinamismo plastico*) (Futurist painting and sculpture [plastic dynamism]) appeared in 1914. In July 1915 Boccioni enlisted in the army with Marinetti, Russolo, and Antonio Sant'Elia. He suffered an accident during cavalry exercises in Sorte near Verona, Italy, and died on August 17, 1916.

CONSTANTIN BRANCUSI

b. 1876, Hobitza, Romania; d. 1957, Paris

Constantin Brancusi was born on February 19, 1876, in Hobitza, Romania. He studied art at the Scoala de Meserii in Craiova from 1894 to 1898 and at the Scoala Natzionala de Arte Frumoase in Bucharest from 1898 to 1901. Eager to continue his education in Paris, Brancusi arrived there in 1904 and enrolled in the École des Beaux-Arts in 1905. The following year, his sculpture was shown at the Salon d'Automne, where he met Auguste Rodin.

Soon after 1907, Brancusi's mature period began. The sculptor had settled in Paris but throughout these years returned frequently to Bucharest and exhibited there almost every year. In Paris, his friends included Marcel Duchamp, Fernand Léger, Henri Matisse, Amedeo Modigliani, and Henri Rousseau. In 1913, five of Brancusi's sculptures were included in the *International Exhibition of Modern Art* (popularly known as the Armory Show) in New York. Alfred Stieglitz presented the first solo show of Brancusi's work at his gallery 291 in New York in 1914. Brancusi was never a member of any organized artistic movement, although he associated with Francis Picabia, Tristan Tzara, and many other Dadaists in the early 1920s. In 1921, he was honored with a special issue of *Little Review* (1914–29). He traveled to the United States twice in 1926 to attend his solo shows at Wildenstein & Co. and at the Brummer Gallery in New York. The following year, a historic trial was initiated in the United States to determine whether Brancusi's *Bird in Space* (*L'oiseau dans l'espace*, ca. 1923–26) was liable for duty as a manufactured object or as a work of art. The court decided in 1928 that the sculpture was a work of art.

Brancusi traveled extensively in the 1930s, visiting India and Egypt as well as European countries. He was commissioned to create a war memorial for a park in Târgu Jiu, Romania, in 1935, and designed a complex that included gates, tables, stools, and his work *Endless Column*. After 1939, Brancusi continued to work in Paris. His last sculpture, a plaster *Grand Coq*, was completed in 1949. In 1952, Brancusi became a French citizen. He died on March 16, 1957, in Paris.

GEORGES BRAQUE

b. 1882, Argenteuil-sur-Seine, France; d. 1963, Paris

Georges Braque was born on May 13, 1882, in Argenteuil-sur-Seine, France. He grew up in Le Havre and studied evenings at the École des Beaux-Arts there from about 1897 to 1899. He left for Paris to study under a master decorator to receive his craftsman certificate in 1901. From 1902 to 1904 he painted at the Académie Humbert in Paris, where he met Marie Laurencin and Francis Picabia. By 1906 Braque's work was no longer Impressionist but Fauvist in style; after spending that summer in Antwerp with Othon Friesz, he showed his Fauve work the following year in the Salon des Indépendants in Paris. His first solo show was at Daniel-Henry Kahnweiler's gallery in 1908. From 1909 Pablo Picasso and Braque worked together in developing Cubism; by 1911 their styles were extremely similar. In 1912 they started to incorporate collage elements into their paintings and to experiment with the papier collé (pasted paper) technique. Their artistic collaboration lasted until 1914. Braque served in the French army during World War I and was wounded; upon his recovery in 1917, he began a close friendship with Juan Gris.

After World War I Braque's work became freer and less schematic. His fame grew in 1922 as a result of an exhibition at the Salon d'Automne in Paris. In the mid-1920s Braque designed the decor for two Sergei Diaghilev ballets. By the end of the decade, he had returned to a more realistic interpretation of nature, although certain aspects of Cubism always remained present in his work. In 1931 Braque made his first engraved plaster works and began to portray mythological subjects. His first important retrospective took place in 1933 at the Kunsthalle Basel. He won first prize at the Carnegie International, Pittsburgh, in 1937.

During World War II Braque remained in Paris. His paintings at that time, primarily still lifes and interiors, became more somber. In addition to paintings, Braque also made lithographs, engravings, and sculptures. From the late 1940s he treated various recurring themes such as birds, ateliers, landscapes, and seascapes. In 1954 he designed stained-glass windows for the church of Varengeville. During the last few years of his life, Braque's ill health prevented him from undertaking further large-scale commissions, but he continued to paint, make lithographs, and design jewelry. He died on August 31, 1963, in Paris.

CARLO CARRÀ

b. 1881, Quargnento, Italy; d. 1966, Milan

Carlo Carrà was born in Quargnento, Italy, on February 11, 1881. At twelve he left home to work as a mural decorator first in Valenza Po, and from 1895 in Milan. In 1899–1900, Carrà decorated pavilions at the Exposition universelle (Universal Exposition) in Paris, where he became acquainted with contemporary French art. In 1906, he enrolled at the Accademia di Brera in Milan, where he studied under Cesare Tallone.

Carrà met Umberto Boccioni and Luigi Russolo in 1908 and, after his encounter with Filippo Tommaso Marinetti, in February 1910, signed with them the "Manifesto dei pittori futuristi" ("Manifesto of Futurist Painters"), followed in April by the "Manifesto tecnico della pittura futurista" ("Technical Manifesto of Futurist Painting"). Carrà's radical political and artistic interests were combined in the monumental painting *Funeral of the Anarchist Galli* (*I funerali dell'anarchico Galli*, 1910–11). With Ardengo Soffici, Carrà contributed to the Italian Futurist periodical *Lacerba* (1913–15). In 1914, Carrà returned to Paris where he started to work in collage and *parole in libertà* (words-in-freedom), and endorsed the Italian Interventionist movement in his book *Guerrapittura* (War-painting) of 1915.

By 1916, Carrà had rejected many of the nihilistic premises of Futurism. In essays such as "Parlata su Giotto" (Speaking of Giotto), and "Paolo Uccello costruttore" (Paolo Uccello, constructor), published in *La Voce* (1908–16) that year, Carrà exalted the art of the Italian Trecento (1300s) and Quattrocento (1400s) primitives for its clarity of form and spiritual dimension. In 1917, he met Giorgio de Chirico and adapted his metaphysical iconography and compositional techniques to a series of bizarre still lifes and interiors. In 1918, Carrà, de Chirico, and his brother Alberto Savinio joined the magazine *Valori Plastici* (1918–22). The following year, he published his book *Pittura metafisica* (Metaphysical painting), which celebrated the transcendent properties of pure form and commonplace objects. Carrà's theoretical position, grounded in a postwar "return to order," signaled his break with the ironic classicism of de Chirico.

In 1921 Carrà began a seventeen-year tenure as art critic for the Milanese newspaper *L'Ambrosiano* (1922–44). He participated in the two exhibitions of the Novecento italiano (Italian 1900s), while his interest in the indigenous qualities of the Italian landscape drew him close to the regionalist Strapaese group. In the 1930s Carrà received commissions for mural paintings under the regime, and signed Mario Sironi's "Manifesto della pittura murale" ("Manifesto of Mural Painting") in 1933. In 1941 he was appointed professor of painting at the Accademia di Brera. In 1945 he published his autobiography *La mia vita* (My life). Carrà died in Milan on April 13, 1966.

PAUL CÉZANNE

b. 1839, Aix-en-Provence, France; d. 1906, Aix-en-Provence

Paul Cézanne was born on January 19, 1839, in Aix-en-Provence, France. While in school, he enrolled in the free-drawing academy in Aix, which he attended intermittently for several years. In 1858 he graduated from the Collège Bourbon, where he had become an intimate friend of fellow student and future writer Émile Zola. Cézanne entered law school in Aix in 1859 to placate his father but abandoned his studies to join Zola in Paris in 1861. For the next twenty years Cézanne divided his time between the Midi and Paris. While in the capital, he briefly attended the Atelier Suisse with Camille Pissarro, whose art later came to influence his own. In 1862 Cézanne began what would become long friendships with Claude Monet and Pierre-Auguste Renoir. His paintings were included in the 1863 Salon des Refusés, which displayed works not accepted by the jury of the official Paris Salon. The salon itself rejected Cézanne's submissions each year from 1864 to 1869.

Following the declaration of the Franco-Prussian War in 1870, Cézanne left Paris for Aix-en-Provence and then nearby L'Estaque, where he continued to paint. He made the first of several visits to Pontoise, France, in 1872; there, he worked alongside Pissarro. He participated in the first Impressionist exhibition of 1874. From 1876 to 1879 his works were again rejected by the salon. Cézanne showed again with the Impressionists in 1877 in their third exhibition. At that time, Georges Rivière was one of the few critics to support his art. In 1882 the salon accepted his work for the first and only time. Beginning in 1883 Cézanne resided in the south of France, returning to Paris occasionally.

In 1890 Cézanne exhibited with the group Les Vingt (The Twenty) in Brussels and spent five months in Switzerland. He traveled to Giverny in 1894 to visit Monet, who introduced him to Auguste Rodin and the critic Gustave Geffroy. Cézanne's first solo show was held at Ambroise Vollard's gallery in Paris in 1895. From then on he received increasing recognition, and in 1899 he participated in the Salon des Indépendants in Paris for the first time. The following year he took part in the Exposition universelle (Universal Exposition) in Paris. In 1903 the Berliner and Wien Secessions included Cézanne's work, and in 1904 he exhibited at the Salon d'Automne, Paris. That same year he was given a solo exhibition at the Galerie Paul Cassirer, Berlin. Cézanne died on October 22, 1906, in Aix-en-Provence. A posthumous retrospective of his work was held at the Salon d'Automne in 1907.

MARC CHAGALL

b. 1887, Vitebsk, Russia; d. 1985, Saint Paul de Vence, France

Marc Chagall was born on July 7, 1887, in Vitebsk, Russia (now Belarus). From 1907 to 1910 he studied in Saint Petersburg, at the Imperatorskoye Obshchestvo Pooshchreniya Khudozhestv (Imperial Society for the Protection of the Arts), and later with Léon Bakst. In 1910 he moved to Paris, where he associated with Guillaume Apollinaire and Robert Delaunay and encountered Fauvism and Cubism. He participated in the Salon des Indépendants and the Salon d'Automne in 1912. His first solo show was held in 1914 at Herwarth Walden's Der Sturm gallery in Berlin.

Chagall visited Russia in 1914 and was prevented from returning to Paris by the outbreak of war. He settled in Vitebsk, where he was appointed Commissar for Art in 1918. He founded the Vitebskoe Narodnoe Khudozhestvennoe Uchilishche (Vitebsk Popular Art School) in early 1919 and directed it until disagreements with the Suprematists resulted in his resignation in 1920. He moved to Moscow and executed his first stage designs for the Gosudarstvennyi Evreiskii Kamernyi Teatr (GOSEKT) (State Jewish Chamber Theater). After a sojourn in Berlin, Chagall returned to Paris in 1923 and met art dealer Ambroise Vollard. His first retrospective took place in 1924 at the Galerie Barbazanges-Hodebert there. During the 1930s he traveled to Palestine, the Netherlands, Spain, Poland, and Italy. In 1933 the Kunsthalle Basel held a major retrospective of his work.

During World War II Chagall fled to the United States. The Museum of Modern Art, New York, gave him a retrospective in 1946. He settled permanently in France in 1948 and exhibited in Paris, Amsterdam, and London. In 1951 he visited Israel and executed his first sculptures. The following year the artist traveled in Greece and Italy. During the 1960s Chagall continued to travel widely, often in association with large-scale commissions he received. Among these were windows for the synagogue of the Hadassah University Medical Center, Jerusalem (installed in 1962); a ceiling for the Paris Opéra (installed in 1964); a window for the United Nations building, New York (installed in 1964); murals for the Metropolitan Opera House, New York (installed in 1967); and windows for the cathedral in Metz, France (installed in 1968). An exhibition of the artist's work from 1967 to 1977 was held at the Musée du Louvre, Paris, in 1977–78, and a major retrospective was held at the Philadelphia Museum of Art in 1985. Chagall died on March 28, 1985, in Saint Paul de Vence, France.

GIORGIO DE CHIRICO

b. 1888, Vólos, Greece; d. 1978, Rome

Giorgio de Chirico was born to Italian parents in Vólos, Greece, on July 10, 1888. In 1900 he began studies at the polytechnic institute in Athens and attended evening classes in drawing from the nude. Around 1906 he moved to Munich, where he attended the Akademie der bildenden Künste. At this time he became interested in the art of Arnold Böcklin and Max Klinger and the writings of Friedrich Nietzsche and Arthur Schopenhauer. De Chirico moved to Milan in 1909, to Florence in 1910, and to Paris in 1911. In Paris he was included in the Salon d'Automne in 1912 and 1913 and in the Salon des Indépendants in 1913 and 1914. As a frequent visitor to Guillaume Apollinaire's weekly gatherings, he met Constantin Brancusi, André Derain, Max Jacob, and others. Because of the war, in 1915 de Chirico returned to Italy, where he met Filippo de Pisis in 1916 and Carlo Carrà in 1917; they formed the group that was later called the Scuola metafisica (Metaphysical School).

The artist moved to Rome in 1918 and was given his first solo exhibition at the Casa d'arte Bragaglia in that city in the winter of 1918–19. In this period he was one of the leaders of the Valori plastici (Plastic Values) group, with whom he showed at the Nationalgalerie in Berlin. From 1920 to 1924 he divided his time between Rome and Florence. A solo exhibition of de Chirico's work was held at the Galleria

Arte in Milan in 1921, and he participated in the Venice Biennale for the first time in 1924. In 1925 the artist returned to Paris, where he exhibited that year at Léonce Rosenberg's Galerie l'effort moderne. In Paris his work was shown at the Galerie Paul Guillaume in 1926 and 1927 and at the Galerie Jeanne Bucher in 1927. In 1928 he was given solo shows at the Arthur Tooth Gallery in London and the Valentine Gallery in New York. In 1929 de Chirico designed scenery and costumes for Sergei Diaghilev's production of the ballet *Le bal*, and his book *Hebdomeros* was published. The artist designed for the ballet and opera in subsequent years and continued to exhibit in Europe, the United States, Canada, and Japan. In 1945 the first part of his book *Memorie della mia vita* (Memories of my life) appeared. De Chirico died on November 20, 1978, in Rome, his residence for over thirty years.

ROBERT DELAUNAY

b. 1885, Paris; d. 1941, Montpellier, France

Robert Delaunay was born Robert-Victor-Félix Delaunay on April 12, 1885, in Paris. In 1902, after his secondary education, he apprenticed in a studio for theater sets in Belleville, France. In 1903 he started painting and by 1904 was exhibiting. That year and in 1906, his work was shown at the Salon d'Automne and regularly from 1904 until World War I at the Salon des Indépendants. Between 1905 and 1907 Delaunay became friendly with Jean Metzinger and Henri Rousseau and studied the color theories of Michel-Eugène Chevreul. During these years, he painted in a Neo-Impressionist manner; Paul Cézanne's work also influenced Delaunay around this time. From 1907 to 1908 he served in the military in Laon, and upon returning to Paris, he had contact with the Cubists. The period of 1909–10 saw the emergence of Delaunay's personal style; he painted his first *Eiffel Tower* (*Tour Eiffel*) in 1909. In 1910 Delaunay married the painter Sonia Terk, who became his collaborator on many projects.

Delaunay's participation in exhibitions in Germany and his association with advanced artists working there began in 1911, the year Vasily Kandinsky invited him to participate in the first Der Blaue Reiter (The Blue Rider) exhibition at the Moderne Galerie Heinrich Thannhauser in Munich. At this time he became friendly with Guillaume Apollinaire, Albert Gleizes, and Henri Le Fauconnier. In 1912 Delaunay's first solo show took place at the Galerie Barbazanges, Paris, and he began his *Windows* (*Fenêtres*) pictures. In 1913 Delaunay painted his *Circular Forms* (*Formes circulaires*), or *Disc*, pictures.

From 1914 to 1920 Delaunay lived in Spain and Portugal and became friends with Sergei Diaghilev, Léonide Massine, Diego Rivera, and Igor Stravinsky. He designed decor for the Ballets Russes in 1918. In 1920 he returned to Paris, where in 1922 an exhibition of his work was held at Galerie Paul Guillaume. He began his second *Eiffel Tower* (*Tour Eiffel*) series in that same year. In 1924 he undertook his series of *Runners* (*Coureurs*) and in 1925 executed frescoes for the Palais de l'ambassade de France at the Exposition internationale des arts décoratifs (International Exposition of Decorative Arts) in Paris. In 1937 he was commissioned to decorate the Palais des chemins de fer and Palais de l'air at the Paris Exposition internationale (International Exposition). His last works were decorations for the sculpture hall of the Salon des Tuileries in 1938. Delaunay died on October 25, 1941, in Montpellier, France.

ANDRÉ DERAIN

b. 1880, Chatou, France; d. 1954, Garches, France

André Derain was born on June 10, 1880, in Chatou, France. In 1898–99, he attended the Académie Camillo, studied with Eugène Carrière, and met Henri Matisse. In 1900, he met and shared a studio with Maurice de Vlaminck and painted his first landscapes. In 1905, the dealer Ambroise Vollard purchased all the works from Derain's studio. In the same year, Derain exhibited at the Salon des Indépendants, worked with Matisse in Collioure, France, during July and August, painted in L'Estaque and Marseilles, exhibited alongside the other Fauve artists in the Salon d'Automne, and made his first trip to London. Daniel-Henry Kahnweiler became Derain's dealer in 1907. During that year, the artist experimented with stone sculpture and moved to Montmartre, where he associated with Pablo Picasso and other artists and poets at the Bateau-Lavoir. Derain's work of this period manifested an increasingly restrained palette and more tightly woven brushwork in a movement away from his well-known Fauvist style of 1905–07.

Derain spent the spring of 1909 painting in Carrières-Saint-Denis, France, where Georges Braque visited him frequently. The following year, he and Picasso painted together in Cadaqués, Spain. In 1912, Derain developed an interest in the nude and in the following years produced many still lifes. In 1913, Derain's work gained international exposure through his participation in the *International Exhibition of Modern Art* (popularly known as the Armory Show), New York, and the Erster deutscher Herbstsalon (First German Autumn Salon) at Herwarth Walden's Der Sturm gallery, Berlin. He exhibited widely in Germany in 1914. During World War I, Derain served in the military, producing a variety of works at the front, including inventive masks made from shell cases. In 1916, his first solo exhibition was held at the Galerie Paul Guillaume, Paris, for which Guillaume Apollinaire wrote the introduction to the catalogue. In 1919, he collaborated with Sergei Diaghilev, designing the sets and costumes for his production of *La boutique fantasque* in London. Kahnweiler purchased Derain's artistic output from 1920 through 1922, and Paul Guillaume served as his dealer from 1923 until 1934. His work was informed by a wide variety of stylistic precursors, including Florentine painting and the frescoes of Pompeii.

During World War II, Derain went to Berlin with a group of French artists to attend the exhibition of Nazi sculptor Arno Brecker. This visit, for which he was strongly criticized, reflects the culmination of Derain's radical departure from the stylistic and conceptual concerns of the avant-garde in France. Derain died on September 8, 1954, in Garches, France.

MARCEL DUCHAMP

b. 1887, Blainville, France; d. 1968, Neuilly-sur-Seine, France

Marcel Duchamp was born Henri-Robert-Marcel Duchamp on July 28, 1887, near Blainville, France. In 1904, he joined his artist brothers, Jacques Villon and Raymond Duchamp-Villon, in Paris, where he studied painting at the Académie Julian until 1905. Duchamp's early works were Post-Impressionist in style. He exhibited for the first time in 1909 at the Salon des Indépendants and the Salon d'Automne in Paris. His paintings of 1911 were directly related to Cubism but emphasized successive images of a single body in motion. In 1912, he painted the definitive version of *Nude Descending a Staircase* (*Nu descendant un escalier*), which was shown at the Salon de la Section d'Or of that same year and subsequently created great controversy at the *International Exhibition of Modern Art* (popularly known as the Armory Show) in New York in 1913.

Duchamp's radical and iconoclastic ideas predated the founding of the Dada movement in Zurich in 1916. By 1913, he had abandoned traditional painting and drawing for various experimental forms, including mechanical drawings, studies, and notations that would be incorporated in a major work, *The Bride Stripped Bare by Her Bachelors, Even* (*La mariée mise à nu par ses célibataires, même*, 1915–23; also known as *The Large Glass*). In 1914, Duchamp introduced his readymades—common objects, sometimes altered, presented as works of art—which had a revolutionary impact on many painters and sculptors. In 1915, Duchamp traveled to New York, where his circle included Katherine Dreier and Man Ray, with whom he founded the Société Anonyme in 1920, as well as Louise and Walter Arensberg, Francis Picabia, and other avant-garde figures.

After playing chess avidly for nine months in Buenos Aires, Duchamp returned to France in the summer of 1919 and associated with the Dada group in Paris. In New York in 1920, he made his first motor-driven constructions and invented Rrose Sélavy, his feminine alter ego. Duchamp moved back to Paris in 1923 and seemed to have abandoned art for chess but in fact continued his artistic experiments. From the mid-1930s, he collaborated with the Surrealists and participated in their exhibitions. Duchamp settled permanently in New York in 1942 and became a U.S. citizen in 1955. During the 1940s, he associated and exhibited with the Surrealist émigrés in New York, and in 1946 began *Given: 1. The Waterfall, 2. The Illuminating Gas . . .* (*Etant donnés: 1. la chute d'eau 2. le gaz d'éclairage . . .*), a major assemblage on which he worked secretly for the next twenty years. He died on October 2, 1968, in Neuilly-sur-Seine, France.

RAYMOND DUCHAMP-VILLON

b. 1876, Damville, France; d. 1918, Cannes, France

Raymond Duchamp-Villon was born Pierre-Maurice-Raymond Duchamp on November 5, 1876, in Damville, near Rouen, France. From 1894 to 1898 he studied medicine in Paris. When illness forced him to abandon his studies, he decided to make a career in sculpture, until then an avocation. During the early years of the century he moved to Paris, where he exhibited for the first time at the Salon de la Société Nationale des Beaux-Arts in 1902. His second show was held at the same salon in 1903, the year he settled in Neuilly-sur-Seine. In 1905 he had his first exhibition at the Salon d'Automne and a show at the Galerie Legrip in Rouen with his brother, the painter Jacques Villon; he moved with him to Puteaux two years later.

His participation in the jury of the sculpture section of the Salon d'Automne began in 1907 and was instrumental in promoting the Cubists in the early 1910s. Around this time he, Villon, and their other brother, Marcel Duchamp, attended weekly meetings of the Puteaux group of artists and critics. In 1911 he exhibited at the Galerie de l'art contemporain in Paris; the following year his work was included in a show organized by the Duchamp brothers at the Salon de la Section d'Or at the Galerie de la Boétie. Duchamp-Villon's work was exhibited at the *International Exhibition of Modern Art* (popularly known as the Armory Show) in New York in 1913 and the Galerie André Groult in Paris, the Galerie S. V. U. Mánes in Prague, and Herwarth Walden's Der Sturm gallery in Berlin in 1914. During World War I, Duchamp-Villon served in the army in a medical capacity, but was able to continue work on his major sculpture *The Horse* (*Le cheval*, 1914). He contracted typhoid fever in late 1916 while stationed at Champagne; the disease ultimately resulted in his death on October 9, 1918, in the military hospital in Cannes, France.

LYONEL FEININGER

b. 1871, New York; d. 1956, New York

Lyonel Feininger was born Charles Léonell Feininger on July 17, 1871, in New York. At age sixteen he traveled to Germany where he studied drawing at the Kunstgewerbeschule in Hamburg. In 1888 he was admitted to the Kunstakademie in Berlin, which he attended intermittently until 1892. As early as 1889 Feininger's drawings were illustrated in Berlin's humorous weeklies, and by the late 1890s he had become Germany's leading political cartoonist. In the winter of 1903–04, his drawings were exhibited in the Berliner Secession.

In 1906 Feininger moved from Berlin to Paris, where he met Robert Delaunay. The following year he began to paint. In Paris he admired the paintings of Paul Cézanne and Vincent van Gogh, and in London in 1908 was deeply impressed by the work of J. M. W. Turner. From 1908 to 1912 the artist resided in Zehlendorf, near Berlin. His paintings were first exhibited at the 1910 Berliner Secession. In 1911 Feininger was introduced to Cubism at the Salon des Indépendants in Paris, where six of his own paintings were on view. At Franz Marc's invitation he participated in the 1913 Erster deutscher Herbstsalon (First German Autumn Salon) at Herwarth Walden's Der Sturm gallery in Berlin with the artists of Der Blaue Reiter (The Blue Rider) group. Feininger resettled in Berlin for the war years. His first solo show was held at Der Sturm in 1917. The following year he joined the Novembergruppe (November Group) and met Walter Gropius, with whom he traveled to Weimar in 1919 to serve on the faculty of the newly founded Bauhaus. In 1921 Feininger, who was always interested in music, composed the first of his thirteen fugues for the organ. In 1924 he joined Vasily Kandinsky, Paul Klee, and Alexei Jawlensky in the Blue Four group.

Feininger moved with the Bauhaus to Dessau in 1925 but was no longer obligated to teach. In 1929 his work was included in the first show of the Museum of Modern Art in New York, *Paintings by Nineteen Living Americans.* His sixtieth birthday was observed with a retrospective at the Nationalgalerie in Berlin in 1931. In 1936 he taught a summer course at Mills College in Oakland, California, and in 1937 he fled Germany to settle permanently in New York. The following year he was commissioned to design murals for the New York World's Fair. In 1944 he shared a retrospective with Marsden Hartley at the Museum of Modern Art. He taught at Black Mountain College in Black Mountain, North Carolina, during the summer of

1945, and in 1947 was elected president of the Federation of American Painters and Sculptors. Feininger died on January 13, 1956, in New York.

PAUL GAUGUIN

b. 1848, Paris; d. 1903, Marquesas Islands

Paul Gauguin was born on June 7, 1848, in Paris and lived in Lima, Peru, from 1851 to 1855. He served as a merchant marine from 1865 to 1871 and traveled in the tropics. Gauguin later worked as a stockbroker's clerk in Paris but painted in his free time. He began working with Camille Pissarro in 1874 and showed in every Impressionist exhibition between 1879 and 1886. By 1884 Gauguin had moved with his family to Copenhagen, where he unsuccessfully pursued a business career. He returned to Paris in 1885 to paint full-time, leaving his family in Denmark.

In 1885 Gauguin met Edgar Degas; the next year he met Charles Laval and Émile Bernard in Pont-Aven, France, and Vincent van Gogh in Paris. With Laval he traveled to Panama and Martinique in 1887 in search of more exotic subject matter. Increasingly, Gauguin turned to primitive cultures for inspiration. The following year in Brittany, he met Paul Sérusier and renewed his acquaintance with Bernard. As self-designated Synthetists, they were welcomed in Paris by the Symbolist literary and artistic circle. Gauguin organized a group exhibition of their work at the Café Volpini, Paris, in 1889, in conjunction with the Exposition universelle (Universal Exposition).

In 1891 Gauguin auctioned his paintings to raise money for a voyage to Tahiti, which he undertook that same year. Two years later, illness forced him to return to Paris, where, with the critic Charles Morice, he began *Noa Noa*, a book about Tahiti. Gauguin was able to return to Tahiti in 1895. He attempted suicide in January 1898, not long after completing his mural-size painting *Where Do We Come From? What Are We? Where Are We Going?* (*D'ou venons-nous? Que sommes-nous? Où allons-nous?*). In 1899 he championed the cause of French settlers in Tahiti in a political journal, *Les guêpes* (1899–1900), and founded his own periodical, *Le sourire* (1889–1911). Gauguin's other writings include *Cahier pour Aline* (Notebook for Aline, 1892), *L'espirit moderne et le catholicisme* (The modern spirit and catholicism, 1897 and 1902) and *Avant et après* (Before and after, 1902), all of which are autobiographical. In 1901 the artist moved to the Marquesas, where he died on May 8, 1903. A major retrospective of his work was held at the Salon d'Automne in Paris in 1906.

ALBERT GLEIZES

b. 1881, Paris; d. 1953, Avignon, France

Albert Léon Gleizes was born in Paris on December 8, 1881. He worked in his father's fabric design studio after completing secondary school. While serving in the army from 1901 to 1905, Gleizes began to paint seriously. He exhibited for the first time at the Société nationale des beaux-arts, Paris, in 1902, and participated in the Salon d'Automne in 1903 and 1904.

With several friends, including the writer René Arcos, Gleizes founded the Abbaye de Créteil outside Paris in 1906. This utopian community of artists and writers scorned bourgeois society and sought to create a nonallegorical, epic art based on modern themes. The Abbaye closed in 1908 due to financial difficulties. In 1909 and 1910 Gleizes met Robert Delaunay, Henri Le Fauconnier, Fernand Léger, and Jean Metzinger. In 1910 he exhibited at the Salon des Indépendants, Paris, and *Bubnovyi valet* (*Jack of Diamonds*) in Moscow. The following year, he wrote the first of many articles. In collaboration with Metzinger, Gleizes wrote *Du "cubisme"* (*On "Cubism"*), published in 1912. The same year, Gleizes helped found the Section d'Or (Golden Section).

In 1914 Gleizes again saw military service. His paintings had become abstract by 1915, and travels to New York, Barcelona, and Bermuda during the next four years influenced his stylistic evolution. His first solo show was held at the Galeries Dalmau, Barcelona, in 1916. Beginning in 1918 Gleizes became deeply involved in a search for spiritual values, as reflected in his painting and writing. In 1927 he founded Moly-Sabata, another utopian community of artists and craftsmen, in Sablons, France. His book, *La forme et l'histoire* (Form and history), published in 1932, examines Romanesque, Celtic, and non-Western art. In the 1930s Gleizes participated in the Abstraction-Création (Abstraction-Creation) group. Later in his career Gleizes executed several large commissions, including the murals for the Paris Exposition internationale (International Exposition) of 1937. In 1947 a major Gleizes retrospective took place in Lyons at the Chapelle du Lycée Ampère. From 1949 to 1950 Gleizes worked on illustrations for Blaise Pascal's *Pensées sur l'homme et Dieu* (*Thoughts about Man and God*, 1670). He executed a fresco, *Eucharist*, for the chapel Les Fontaines at Chantilly in 1952. Gleizes died in Avignon, France, on June 23, 1953.

NATALIA GONCHAROVA

b. 1881, Nagaevo, Russia; d. 1962, Paris

Natalia Goncharova was born on June 21, 1881, in Nagaevo, Russia. In 1892, she moved to Moscow to attend school. In 1900, she met Mikhail Larionov, who encouraged her to paint and became her lifelong companion. The following year, she enrolled at the Moscow Institute of Painting, Sculpture, and Architecture to study sculpture. Goncharova participated in an exhibition of Russian artists organized by Sergei Diaghilev at the 1906 Salon d'Automne in Paris. Her early work shows the influence of Impressionism, Fauvism, and Russian folk sculpture.

Goncharova participated in numerous important exhibitions of new art in Moscow, including *Bubnovyi valet* (*Jack of Diamonds*, 1910), *Oslinyi khvost* (*Donkey's Tail*, 1912), and *Mishen* (*Target*, 1913). While her early works were painted in Primitivist and Cubist styles, she adopted a Cubo-Futurist and Rayist approach around 1912. Goncharova was represented at the second Blaue Reiter (Blue Rider) exhibition at Galerie Hans Goltz, Munich, in 1912 and the Erster deutscher Herbstsalon (First German Autumn Salon) at Herwarth Walden's Der Sturm gallery in Berlin in 1913. Around this time, Goncharova and Larionov began their collaboration with Diaghilev and his Ballets Russes, which lasted until the impresario's death in 1929. In 1917, they settled permanently in Paris, and the following year their work appeared in the exhibition *L'art décoratif théâtral moderne* (*Modern Theatrical Decorative Art*) at the Galerie Sauvage, Paris.

Goncharova showed extensively during the 1920s and 1930s, often with Larionov, in Europe, the United States, and Japan. Although she never abandoned painting, much of her creative energy was directed toward stage decoration and book illustration. She designed costumes, settings, and drop curtains for international presentations of modern and classical ballets until she was in her seventies. In 1938, Goncharova became a French citizen, and in 1955 she married Larionov. The following year, she was given a retrospective at the Galerie de l'institut in Paris. Goncharova died on October 17, 1962, in Paris.

OTTO GUTFREUND

b. 1889, Dvůr Králové, Austria-Hungary; d. 1927, Prague

Otto Gutfreund was born on August 3, 1889, in Dvůr Králové, Austria-Hungary (now Czech Republic). After attending a ceramics school in Bechyně, he spent three years at the Uměleckoprumyslová škola (School of Decorative Arts) in Prague. During 1909–10, Gutfreund worked in the Paris studio of Emile Antoine Bourdelle and attended his sculpture class at the Académie de la Grande Chaumière.

He returned to Prague and in 1911 cofounded the Skupina výtvarných umělců (Group of Plastic Artists). This diverse group of artists, architects, writers, and musicians was closely aligned with the French Cubists and also Die Brücke (The Bridge) artists in Germany, who encountered the Czech avant-garde during their 1910 visit to Prague. The Skupina výtvarných umělců organized four exhibitions at Prague's town hall between 1912 and 1914. As the sole sculptor, Gutfreund participated in all four presentations and contributed to the group's journal, *Umělecký měslčnik* (1911–14). Gutfreund also helped establish international contacts for the group, leading to its participation in the 1913 Erster deutscher Herbstsalon (First German Autumn Salon) at Herwarth Walden's Der Sturm gallery in Berlin. That same year the Czech group exhibited again at Der Sturm and at Galerie Hans Goltz in Munich.

Gutfreund went to Paris in the spring of 1914. He joined the Foreign Legion after the outbreak of World War I, serving as a member of the Czechoslovak Nazdar unit. In late 1915 the artist was interned in a camp in Provence for alleged incitement to rebellion (he protested conditions within the legion). He resumed his artistic activities in 1920 in Prague, joining the association Spolek výtvarných umělců Mánes (S.V.U. Mánes) (Mánes Union of Artists) the following year. Gutfreund also completed a number of public commissions for the new Czechoslovak Republic. In the mid-1920s, the artist returned to a more abstract style in his sculpture and joined the faculty at Prague's School of Decorative Arts. Gutfreund drowned on June 2, 1927, while swimming in the River Vltava in Prague.

JUAN GRIS

b. 1887, Madrid; d. 1927, Boulogne-sur-Seine, France

Juan Gris was born José Victoriano Carmelo Carlos González-Pérez in Madrid on March 23, 1887. He studied mechanical drawing at the Escuela de Artes y Manufacturas in Madrid from 1902 to 1904, during which time he contributed drawings to local periodicals. From 1904 to 1905 he studied painting with the academic artist José Maria Carbonero. In 1906 he moved to Paris, where he lived for most of the remainder of his life. His friends in Paris included Georges Braque, Fernand Léger, and Pablo Picasso as well as the writers Guillaume Apollinaire, Max Jacob, and Maurice Raynal. Although he continued to submit humorous illustrations to journals such as *L'assiette au beurre* (1901–12), *Le charivari* (1832–1937), and *Le cri de Paris* (1897–?), Gris began to paint seriously in 1910. By 1912 he had developed a personal Cubist style.

He exhibited for the first time in 1912 at the Salon des Indépendants in Paris, Galeries Dalmau in Barcelona, Der Sturm gallery in Berlin, the Salon de la Société Normande de Peinture Moderne in Rouen, and the Salon de la Section d'Or in Paris. That same year Daniel-Henry Kahnweiler signed Gris to a contract that gave Kahnweiler exclusive rights to the artist's work. Gris became a good friend of Henri Matisse in 1914 and over the next several years formed close relationships with Jacques Lipchitz and Jean Metzinger. After Kahnweiler fled Paris at the outbreak of World War I, Gris signed a contract with art dealer Léonce Rosenberg in 1916. His first major solo show was held at Rosenberg's Galerie l'effort moderne in Paris in 1919. The following year Kahnweiler returned and once again became Gris's dealer.

In 1922 the painter first designed ballet sets and costumes for Sergei Diaghilev. Gris articulated most of his aesthetic theories during 1924 and 1925. He delivered his definitive lecture, "Des possibilités de la peinture" (The possibilities of painting), at the Sorbonne in 1924. Major Gris exhibitions took place at Kahnweiler's Galerie Simon in Paris and the Galerie Flechtheim in Berlin in 1923 and at the Galerie Flechtheim in Düsseldorf in 1925. As his health declined, Gris made frequent visits to the south of France. He died in Boulogne-sur-Seine, France, on May 11, 1927.

ALEXEI JAWLENSKY

b. 1864, Torzhok, Russia; d. 1941, Wiesbaden, Germany

Alexei Georgevich Jawlensky was born near Torzhok, Russia, on March 13, 1864, and educated in Moscow. While an army lieutenant, he first studied art at the academy in Saint Petersburg in 1889. In 1896 Jawlensky resigned from his military commission to devote himself to painting and moved with Marianne von Werefkin and Helene Nesnakomoff to Munich. From 1896 to 1899 he attended the Azhbe school in Munich, where he first met Vasily Kandinsky who had also recently left Russia.

Jawlensky was included in the München and Berliner Secession exhibitions in 1903. During the following years he visited Russia, participating in exhibitions there, and traveled in Europe: in 1905 he met Henri Matisse in Paris, and his work was included in the Salon d'Automne. In 1907 he met Nabis (Prophets) members Paul Sérusier and Jan Verkade in Munich. Jawlensky and Kandinsky became close friends during the summer of 1908 and the following year the two, together with a number of other artists, founded the Neue Künstlervereinigung München (NKVM) (New Artists' Association of Munich). Jawlensky's first solo exhibition took place in Barmen, Germany, in 1911. His long friendship with Emil Nolde began in 1912.

The outbreak of World War I forced Jawlensky to flee to Switzerland, where he painted his stylized landscape series, *Variations* (*Variationen*), from 1914 to 1921. In Zurich in 1917 he started his two most well-known series, the *Mystical Heads* (*Mystische Köpfe*, 1917–19), and the *Saviour's Faces* (*Heilandsgesichter*, 1917–21), and in Ascona, Switzerland, in 1918 he began his Constructivist heads. Jawlensky returned to Germany in 1921, settling in

Wiesbaden. He married Nesnakomoff, the mother of his twenty-year-old son, in 1922. With Paul Klee, Kandinsky, and Lyonel Feininger he was part of the Blue Four, founded in 1924. Jawlensky continued to paint Constructivist heads during the years in Wiesbaden; from 1934 to 1937 he executed his mystical *Meditations* (*Meditationen*) series. Crippled by arthritis, Jawlensky was finally forced to cease painting by 1938. He died on March 15, 1941, in Wiesbaden.

VASILY KANDINSKY

b. 1866, Moscow; d. 1944, Neuilly-sur-Seine, France

Vasily Kandinsky was born on December 4, 1866, in Moscow. From 1886 through 1892 he studied law and economics at the University of Moscow, where he lectured after graduation. In 1896 he declined a teaching position in order to study art in Munich with Anton Azhbe from 1897 to 1899 and at the Kunstakademie with Franz von Stuck in 1900. Kandinsky taught from 1901 to 1903 at the art school of the Phalanx, a group he cofounded in Munich. One of his students, Gabriele Münter, would be his companion until 1914. In 1902 Kandinsky exhibited for the first time with the Berliner Secession and produced his first woodcuts. In 1903 and 1904 he began his travels in Italy, the Netherlands, and North Africa and his visits to Russia. He showed at the Salon d'Automne in Paris from 1904.

In 1909 Kandinsky was elected president of the newly founded Neue Künstlervereinigung München (NKVM) (New Artists' Association of Munich). The group's first show took place at the Moderne Galerie Heinrich Thannhauser in Munich in 1909. Kandinsky's major aesthetic treatise *Über das Geistige in der Kunst* (*On the Spiritual in Art*) was published in December 1911 (though dated 1912). In that month, Kandinsky and Franz Marc withdrew from the NKVM and formed Der Blaue Reiter (The Blue Rider) group. Shortly thereafter the Blaue Reiter's first exhibition was held at the Moderne Galerie. The two artists had already begun to make plans for *Der Blaue Reiter* (*The Blaue Reiter Almanac*), although the publication would not appear until the following year. In 1912 the second Blaue Reiter show was held at Galerie Hans Goltz, Munich. Kandinsky's first solo show was held at Herwarth Walden's Der Sturm gallery in Berlin in 1912. In 1913 one of his works was included in the *International Exhibition of Modern Art* (popularly known as the Armory Show) in New York and the Erster deutscher Herbstsalon (First German Autumn Salon) at Der Sturm. Kandinsky lived in Russia from 1914 to 1921, principally in Moscow, where he held a position in the IZO-Narkompros (IZO NKP) (Department of Art in the People's Commissariat for Enlightenment).

Kandinsky began teaching at the Bauhaus in Weimar in 1922. In 1923 he was given his first solo show in New York by the Société Anonyme, of which he became vice-president. Lyonel Feininger, Alexei Jawlensky, Kandinsky, and Paul Klee made up the Blue Four group, formed in 1924. He moved with the Bauhaus to Dessau in 1925 and became a German citizen in 1928. The Nazi government closed the Bauhaus in 1933 and later that year Kandinsky settled in Neuilly-sur-Seine, near Paris; he acquired French citizenship in 1939. Fifty-seven of his works were confiscated from German museums by the Nazis in the 1937 purge of so-called *entartete kunst* (degenerate art). Kandinsky died on December 13, 1944, in Neuilly-sur-Seine, France.

ERNST LUDWIG KIRCHNER

b. 1880, Aschaffenburg, Germany; d. 1938, Frauenkirch, Switzerland

Ernst Ludwig Kirchner was born on May 6, 1880, in Aschaffenburg, Germany. After years of travel, his family settled in Chemnitz in 1890. From 1901 to 1905 he studied architecture at the Dresden Technische Hochschule, and pictorial art in Munich at the Kunsthochschule and at an experimental art school established by Wilhelm von Debschitz and Hermann Obrist. While in Munich he produced his first woodcuts; the graphic arts were to become as important to him as painting. At that time he was drawn to Neo-Impressionism as well as to the old masters.

In 1905 the group Die Brücke (The Bridge) was founded in Dresden by Fritz Bleyl, Erich Heckel, Kirchner, and Karl Schmidt-Rottluff; later, Cuno Amiet, Otto Müller, Emil Nolde, and Max Pechstein joined the group. From 1905 to 1910 Dresden hosted exhibitions of Post-Impressionism, including the work of Vincent van Gogh, as well as shows featuring Gustav Klimt, Edvard Munch, and the Fauves, who deeply impressed Kirchner. Other important influences were Japanese prints, and African and Oceanic art. Kirchner moved to Berlin with the Brücke in 1911. The following year Franz Marc included works by Brücke artists in the second show of Der Blaue Reiter (The Blue Rider) group at Galerie Hans Goltz in Munich, thus providing a link between the two associations. In 1913 Kirchner exhibited in the *International Exhibition of Modern Art* (popularly known as the Armory Show) in New York, and was given his first solo shows in Germany at the Museum Folkwang Hagen, and the Galerie Gurlitt, Berlin. That year also marked the dissolution of the Brücke.

During World War I Kirchner was discharged from the army because of a nervous and physical collapse. He was treated at Oskar Kohnstamm's sanatorium in Königstein near Frankfurt, where he completed five wall frescoes in 1916. The artist was severely injured when struck by an automobile in 1917. The next year he settled in Frauenkirch near Davos, Switzerland, where many young artists, particularly those of the Basel-based Rot-Blau (Red-Blue) group, sought him out for guidance. Solo shows of Kirchner's work were held throughout the 1930s in Basel, Bern, Hamburg, Munich, Detroit, and New York. However, physical deterioration and mental anxiety overtook him again in the middle of the decade. His inclusion in *Entartete Kunst*, the Nazis' 1937 exhibition of so-called degenerate art, caused him further distress. Kirchner died by his own hand on June 15, 1938, in Frauenkirch.

PAUL KLEE

b. 1879, Münchenbuchsee, Switzerland;
d. 1940, Muralto-Locarno, Switzerland

Paul Klee was born on December 18, 1879, in Münchenbuchsee, Switzerland, into a family of musicians. His childhood love of music was always to remain profoundly important in his life and work. From 1898 to 1901 Klee studied in Munich, first with Heinrich Knirr, then at the Kunstakademie under Franz von Stuck. Upon completing his schooling, he traveled to Italy. It was the first in a series of trips abroad that nourished his visual sensibilities. He settled in Bern in 1902. A series of his satirical etchings was exhibited at the München Secession in 1906. That same year Klee married Lily Stumpf, a pianist, and moved to Munich. There he gained exposure to modern art. Klee's work was shown at the Kunstmuseum Bern in 1910 and at the Moderne Galerie Heinrich Thannhauser, Munich, in 1911.

Klee met Alexei Jawlensky, Vasily Kandinsky, August Macke, Franz Marc, and other avant-garde figures in 1911; he participated in important shows of advanced art, including the second Blaue Reiter (Blue Rider) exhibition, at Galerie Hans Goltz, Munich, in 1912, and the Erster deutscher Herbstsalon (First German Autumn Salon) at Herwarth Walden's Der Sturm gallery, Berlin, in 1913. In 1912 he visited Paris for the second time, where he saw the work of Georges Braque and Pablo Picasso, and met Robert Delaunay. Klee helped found the Neue Münchner Secession (New Munich Secession) in 1914. Color became central to his art only after a revelatory trip to Tunisia in 1914.

In 1920 a major Klee retrospective was held at Galerie Hans Goltz; his *Schöpferische Konfession* (Creative credo) was published; he was also appointed to the faculty of the Bauhaus. Klee taught at the Bauhaus in Weimar from 1921 to 1926 and in Dessau from 1926 to 1931. During his tenure, he was in close contact with other Bauhaus masters such as Kandinsky and Lyonel Feininger. In 1924 the Blue Four was founded, consisting of Feininger, Jawlensky, Kandinsky, and Klee. Among his notable exhibitions of this period were his first in the United States at the Société Anonyme, New York, in 1924; his first major show in Paris the following year at the Galerie Vavin-Raspail; and an exhibition at the Museum of Modern Art, New York, in 1930. Klee went to Düsseldorf to teach at the academy in 1931, shortly before the Nazis closed the Bauhaus. Forced by the Nazis to leave his position in Düsseldorf in 1933, Klee settled in Bern the following year. Seventeen of his works were included in the Nazi exhibition of so-called degenerate art, *Entartete Kunst*, in 1937. Major Klee exhibitions took place in Bern and Basel in 1935 and in Zurich in 1940. Klee died on June 29, 1940, in Muralto-Locarno, Switzerland.

OSKAR KOKOSCHKA

b. 1886, Pöchlarn, Austria; d. 1980, Montreux, Switzerland

Oskar Kokoschka was born on March 1, 1886, in the Austrian town of Pöchlarn. He spent most of his youth in Vienna, where he entered the Kunstgewerbeschule in 1904 or 1905. While still a student, he painted fans and postcards for the Wiener Werkstätte, which published his first book of poetry in 1908. That same year, Kokoschka was fiercely criticized for the works he exhibited in the Vienna Kunstschau and consequently was dismissed from the Kunstgewerbeschule. At this time, he attracted the attention of the architect Adolf Loos, who became his most vigorous supporter. In this early period, Kokoschka wrote plays that are considered among the first examples of Expressionist drama.

His first solo show was held at the Galerie Paul Cassirer, Berlin, in 1910, followed later that year by another at the Museum Folkwang Essen. In 1910, he also began to contribute to Herwarth Walden's periodical *Der Sturm* (1910–32). Kokoschka concentrated on portraiture, dividing his time between Berlin and Vienna from 1910 to 1914. In 1915, shortly after the outbreak of World War I, he volunteered for a cavalry regiment and served on the eastern front, where he was seriously wounded. Still recuperating in 1917, he settled in Dresden and in 1919 accepted a professorship at the academy there. In 1918, Paul Westheim's comprehensive monograph on the artist was published.

Kokoschka traveled extensively during the 1920s and 1930s in Europe, North Africa, and the Middle East. In 1931 he returned to Vienna but, as a result of the Nazis' growing power, he moved to Prague in 1935. He acquired Czechoslovak citizenship two years later. Kokoschka painted a portrait of Czechoslovakia's president Tomáš Garrigue Masaryk in 1936, and the two became friends. In 1937, the Nazis condemned his work as *entartete kunst* (degenerate art) and removed it from public view in Germany. The artist fled to England in 1938, the year of his first solo show in the United States at Curt Valentin's Buchholz Gallery in New York. In 1947, he became a British national. Two important traveling shows of Kokoschka's work originated in Boston and Munich in 1948 and 1950, respectively. In 1953, he settled in Villeneuve, near Geneva, and began teaching at the Internationale Sommer Akademie für bildenden Künste, where he initiated his Schule des Sehens. Kokoschka's collected writings were published in 1956, and around this time he became involved in stage design. In 1962, he was honored with a retrospective at the Tate Gallery, London. Kokoschka died on February 22, 1980, in Montreux, Switzerland.

FRANTIŠEK KUPKA

b. 1871, Opočno, Austria-Hungary; d. 1957, Puteaux, France

František Kupka was born on September 23, 1871, in Opočno in Austria-Hungary (now Czech Republic). From 1889 to 1892 he studied at the Akademie výtvarných uměni (Academy of Fine Arts). During this time he painted historical and patriotic themes. In 1892, Kupka enrolled at the Akademie der bildenden Künste, Vienna, where he concentrated on symbolic and allegorical subjects. He exhibited at the Kunstverein, Vienna, in 1894. His involvement with theosophy and Eastern philosophy dates from this period. By spring 1896 Kupka had settled in Paris; there he attended the Académie Julian briefly and then studied with Jean-Pierre Laurens at the École des Beaux-Arts.

Kupka worked as an illustrator of books and posters and, during his early years in Paris, became known for his satirical drawings for newspapers and magazines. In 1906 he settled in Puteaux, a suburb of Paris, and that same year exhibited for the first time at the Salon d'Automne. Kupka was deeply impressed by the first Futurist manifesto, published in the Parisian newspaper *Le Figaro* in 1909. Kupka's work became increasingly abstract around 1910–11, reflecting his theories of motion, color, and the relationship between music and painting. In 1911 he attended meetings of the Puteaux group. In 1912 he exhibited at the Salon des Indépendants in the Cubist room, although he did not wish to be identified with any movement.

Tvoření v umění výtvarném (Creation in art), a book Kupka completed in 1913, was published in Prague in 1923. In 1921 his first solo show in Paris was held at Galerie Povolozky. In 1931 he became a founding member of Abstraction-Création (Abstration-Creation) together with Jean Arp, Albert Gleizes, Jean Hélion, Auguste Herbin, Theo van Doesburg, and Georges Vantongerloo. In 1936 his work was included in the exhibition *Cubism and Abstract Art* at the Museum of Modern Art, New York, and in an important show with

Alphonse Mucha at the Jeu de Paume, Paris. A retrospective of his work took place at the Galerie S.V.U. Mánes in Prague in 1946. That same year Kupka participated in the Salon des Réalités Nouvelles, Paris, where he continued to exhibit regularly until his death. During the early 1950s he gained general recognition and had several solo shows in New York. Kupka died in Puteaux, France, on June 24, 1957. Retrospectives were held at the Musée national d'art moderne, Paris, in 1958 and at the Solomon R. Guggenheim Museum, New York, in 1975.

MIKHAIL LARIONOV

b. 1881, Tiraspol, Moldova; d. 1964, Fontenay-aux-Roses, France

Mikhail Larionov was born on May 22, 1881, in Tiraspol, Moldova. From 1898 to 1908, he studied at the Moscow Institute of Painting, Sculpture, and Architecture, where he met Natalia Goncharova; the two lived and worked together until her death in 1962. In 1906, he visited Paris with Sergei Diaghilev, who included Larionov's work in the exhibition of Russian artists at the Salon d'Automne that year. In 1907, the artist abandoned the Impressionism of his previous work for a neoprimitive style inspired by Russian folk art. With David and Vladimir Burliuk and others, he formed the Golubaia roza (Blue Rose) group, under whose auspices the review *Zolotoe runo* (1906–10) was published. The first *Zolotoe runo* (*Golden Fleece*) exhibition of 1908 in Moscow introduced many modern French masters to the Russian public. Larionov also organized the avant-garde *Zveno* (*Link*) and *Oslinyi khvost* (*Donkey's Tail*) exhibitions of 1908 and 1912, respectively, and cofounded the Bubnovyi valet (Jack of Diamonds) group with Aristarkh Lentulov in 1910.

In 1911, he developed a personal abstract style that would later be known as Rayism. An amalgam of Cubism and Italian Futurism, with an emphasis on dynamic, linear light rays, Rayism received its public debut at the *Mishen* (*Target*) exhibition of 1913. That same year, Larionov's manifesto *Luchizm* (*Rayism*) was published in Moscow. The artist also participated in the Erster deutscher Herbstsalon (First German Autumn Salon) at Herwarth Walden's Der Sturm gallery, Berlin, in 1913, and the following year organized the exhibition *No. 4* in Moscow. In May 1914, Larionov and Goncharova accompanied Diaghilev's Ballets Russes to Paris; there Larionov associated with Guillaume Apollinaire. Larionov returned to Russia in July right before the outbreak of World War I and served at the front until his demobilization for health reasons. He then rejoined Diaghilev in Switzerland and devoted himself almost exclusively to designing sets and costumes for the Ballets Russes. After Diaghilev died in 1929, Larionov organized a retrospective of maquettes, costumes, and decor for his ballets at the Galerie Billiet in Paris in 1930, at which time he published *Les Ballets Russes de Diaghilev* (Diaghilev's Russian ballets) with Goncharova and Pierre Vorms.

In 1938, Larionov became a French citizen. He and Goncharova were given a number of joint exhibitions throughout their careers, among them retrospectives in Paris at the Galerie des deux-îles in 1948, the Galerie de l'institut in 1952, and the Musée national d'art moderne in 1963. A solo exhibition of Larionov's work was held in 1956 at the Galerie de l'institut. Larionov died on May 10, 1964, at Fontenay-aux-Roses, France.

FERNAND LÉGER

b. 1881, Argentan, France; d. 1955, Gif-sur-Yvette, France

Joseph Fernand Henri Léger was born on February 4, 1881, in Argentan, France. After apprenticing with an architect in Caen, France, from 1897 to 1899, Léger settled in Paris in 1900 and supported himself as an architectural draftsman. He was refused entrance to the École des Beaux-Arts but nevertheless attended classes there beginning in 1903; he also studied at the Académie Julian. Léger's earliest known works, which date from 1905, were primarily influenced by Impressionism. The experience of seeing the Paul Cézanne retrospective at the Salon d'Automne in 1907 and his contact with the early Cubism of Pablo Picasso and Georges Braque had an extremely significant impact on the development of his personal style. From 1911 to 1914 Léger's work became increasingly abstract, and he started to limit his color to the primaries and black and white. In 1912 he was given his first solo show at Galerie Kahnweiler, Paris.

Léger served in the military from 1914 to 1917. His "mechanical" period, in which figures and objects are characterized by tubular, machinelike forms, began in 1917. During the early 1920s he collaborated with the writer Blaise Cendrars on films and designed sets and costumes for performances by Rolf de Maré's Ballets Suédois; in 1924 he completed his first film, *Ballet mécanique* (*Mechanical Ballet*), which was neither abstract nor narrative but a series of seemingly unrelated images (a woman's teeth and lips, machines, ordinary objects, and routine human activities). Léger opened an atelier with Amédée Ozenfant in 1924 and in 1925 presented his first murals at Le Corbusier's Pavillon de l'esprit nouveau at the Exposition internationale des arts décoratifs (International Exhibition of Decorative Art). In 1931 he visited the United States for the first time. In 1935 the Museum of Modern Art, New York, and the Art Institute of Chicago presented an exhibition of his work. Léger lived in the United States from 1940 to 1945 but returned to France after the war. In the decade before his death, Léger's wide-ranging projects included book illustrations, monumental figure paintings and murals, stained-glass windows, mosaics, polychrome ceramic sculptures, and set and costume designs. In 1955 he won the Grand Prize at the Bienal de São Paulo. Léger died on August 17 of that year at his home in Gif-sur-Yvette, France. The Musée Fernand Léger was inaugurated in 1960 in Gif-sur-Yvette, France.

JACQUES LIPCHITZ

b. 1891, Druskieniki, Lithuania; d. 1973, Capri

Chaim Jacob Lipchitz was born on August 22, 1891, in Druskieniki, Lithuania. At eighteen he moved to Paris, where he attended the École des Beaux-Arts and the Académie Julian and soon met Georges Braque, Juan Gris, and Pablo Picasso. In 1912 he began exhibiting at the Salon National des Beaux-Arts and the Salon d'Automne. Lipchitz's first solo show was held at Léonce Rosenberg's Galerie l'effort moderne in Paris in 1920. Two years later he executed five bas-reliefs for the Barnes Foundation in Merion, Pennsylvania. In 1924 the artist became a French citizen and the following year moved to Boulogne-sur-Seine. He received a commission from the viscount Charles de Noailles for his 1927 sculpture *Joy of Life* (*Joie de vivre*).

Lipchitz's first important retrospective took place at Jeanne Bucher's Galerie de la Renaissance in Paris in 1930. The Brummer Gallery in New York hosted his first large show in the United States in 1935. In 1941 Lipchitz fled Paris for New York, where he began exhibiting regularly at the Buchholz Gallery (later the Curt Valentin Gallery). He settled in Hastings-on-Hudson, New York, in 1947. In 1954 a Lipchitz retrospective traveled from the Museum of Modern Art in New York to the Walker Art Center in Minneapolis and the Cleveland Museum of Art. In 1958 Lipchitz collaborated with the architect Philip Johnson on the Roofless Church in New Harmony, Indiana. This same year he became a U.S. citizen. He visited Israel for the first time in 1963. From 1964 to 1966 Lipchitz showed annually at the Marlborough-Gerson Gallery in New York. Beginning in 1963 he spent several months of each year casting in Pietrasanta, Italy.

From 1970 until 1973, Lipchitz worked on large-scale commissions for the Municipal Plaza in Philadelphia, Columbia University in New York, and the Hadassah Medical Center near Jerusalem. These projects were completed after his death by his wife Yulla. Lipchitz died on May 26, 1973, on Capri.

KAZIMIR MALEVICH

b. 1878, near Kiev; d. 1935, Leningrad

Kazimir Severinovich Malevich was born on February 26, 1878, near Kiev. He studied at the Moscow Institute of Painting, Sculpture, and Architecture in 1903. During the early years of his career, he experimented with various modernist styles and participated in avant-garde exhibitions, such as those of the Moskovskoe Tovarischestvo Khudozhnikov (Moscow Artists' Association), which included Vasily Kandinsky and Mikhail Larionov, and the *Bubnovyi valet* (*Jack of Diamonds*) exhibition of 1910 in Moscow. Malevich showed his primitivist paintings of peasants at the exhibition *Oslinyi khvost* (*Donkey's Tail*) in 1912. After this exhibition he broke with Larionov's group. In 1913, with composer Mikhail Matyushin and writer Alexei Kruchenykh, Malevich drafted a manifesto for the First Futurist Congress. That same year he designed the sets and costumes for the opera *Pobeda nad solnstem* (*Victory over the Sun*) by Matyushin and Kruchenykh. Malevich showed at the Salon des Indépendants in Paris in 1914.

At the exhibition *Posledniaia futuristicheskaya vystavka kartin, "0.10" (nul-desat)* (*The Last Futurist Exhibition of Paintings, "0.10" [Zero-Ten]*) in Petrograd (now Saint Petersburg) in 1915, Malevich introduced his nonobjective, geometric Suprematist paintings. Following the Russian Revolution in 1917, Malevich and other advanced artists were encouraged by the Soviet government and attained prominent administrative and teaching positions. In 1919 he began to explore the three-dimensional applications of Suprematism in architectural models. Malevich began teaching at the Practical Art Institute, Vitebsk, in 1919; he soon became its director. In 1919–20, he was given a solo show, *16-aja Gos. Vystavka: Personal'naja Vystakva K. S. Malevica, Ego Put'ot Impressionizma k Suprematizmu* (*Sixteenth State Exhibition: K. S. Malevich, His Path from Impressionism to Suprematism*) in Moscow, which focused on Suprematism and other nonobjective styles. Malevich and his students at Vitebsk formed the Suprematist group Utverditeli novogo iskusstva (UNOVIS) (Affirmers of the New Art). From 1922 to 1927 he taught at the Institut khudozhestvennoi kultury (INKhUK) (Institute of Artistic Culture) in Petrograd, and between 1924 and 1926 he worked primarily on architectural models with his students.

In 1927 Malevich traveled with an exhibition of his paintings to Warsaw and also went to Berlin, where his work was shown at the *Große Berliner Kunstausstellung* (*Great Berlin Art Exhibition*). In Germany he met Jean Arp, Le Corbusier, Naum Gabo, and Kurt Schwitters and visited the Bauhaus, where he met Walter Gropius. The Tretyakov Gallery in Moscow gave Malevich a solo exhibition in 1929. Because of his connections with German artists, he was arrested in Russia in 1930 and many of his manuscripts were destroyed. In his final period, he painted in a representational style. Malevich died on May 15, 1935, in Leningrad (now Saint Petersburg).

FRANZ MARC

b. 1880, Munich; d. 1916, Verdun-sur-Meuse, France

Franz Marc was born on February 8, 1880, in Munich. The son of a landscape painter, he decided to become an artist after a year of military service interrupted his plans to study philology. From 1900 to 1902 he studied at the Kunstakademie in Munich with Gabriel von Hackl and Wilhelm von Diez. The following year, during a visit to France, he was introduced to Japanese woodcuts and the work of the Impressionists in Paris.

Marc suffered from severe depression from 1904 to 1907. In 1907 he went again to Paris, where he responded enthusiastically to the work of Paul Gauguin, Vincent van Gogh, the Cubists, and the Expressionists; later, he was impressed by the work of Henri Matisse and the Fauves, which he had seen exhibited in 1910. During this period he received steady income from the animal anatomy lessons he gave to artists.

In 1910 Marc's first solo show was held at the Kunsthandlung Brackl, Munich, and he met August Macke and the collector Bernhard Koehler. He publicly defended the Neue Künstlervereinigung München (NKVM) (New Artists' Association of Munich) and was formally welcomed into the group early in 1911, when he met Vasily Kandinsky. After internal dissension split the NKVM, he and Kandinsky formed Der Blaue Reiter (The Blue Rider) group, whose first exhibition took place in December 1911 at the Moderne Galerie. Marc invited members of the Berlin Die Brücke (The Bridge) group to participate in the second Blaue Reiter show two months later at Galerie Hans Goltz, Munich. *Der Blaue Reiter* (*The Blaue Reiter Almanac*) was published with lead articles by Marc in May 1912. When World War I broke out in August 1914, Marc immediately enlisted. He was deeply troubled by Macke's death in action shortly thereafter. During the war, he produced his *Sketchbook from the Field* (*Skizzenbuch aus dem Felde*, 1915). Marc died on March 4, 1916, near Verdun-sur-Meuse, France.

HENRI MATISSE

b. 1869, Le Cateau-Cambrésis, France; d. 1954, Nice

Henri Matisse was born Henri-Émile-Benoît Matisse on December 31, 1869, in Le Cateau-Cambrésis, France. He grew up in Bohain-en-Vermandois and studied law in Paris from 1887 to 1888. By 1891 he had abandoned law and started to paint. In Paris Matisse studied art briefly at the Académie Julian and then at the École des Beaux-Arts with Gustave Moreau.

In 1901 Matisse exhibited at the Salon des Indépendants in Paris and met another future leader of the Fauve movement, Maurice de Vlaminck. His first solo show took place at the Galerie Vollard in 1904. Gertrude and Leo Stein, as well as Etta and Claribel Cone, began to collect Matisse's work at that time. Like many avant-garde artists in Paris, Matisse was receptive to a broad range of influences. He was one of the first painters to take an interest in "primitive" art. Matisse abandoned the palette of the Impressionists and established his characteristic style, with its flat, brilliant color and fluid line. His subjects were primarily women, interiors, and still lifes. In 1913 his work was included in the *International Exhibition of Modern Art* (popularly known as the Armory Show) in New York. By 1923 two Russians, Sergei Shchukin and Ivan Morozov, had purchased nearly fifty of his paintings.

From the early 1920s until 1939, Matisse divided his time primarily between the south of France and Paris. During this period, he worked on paintings, sculptures, lithographs, and etchings; as well as on murals for the Barnes Foundation in Merion, Pennsylvania; designs for tapestries; and set and costume designs for Léonide Massine's ballet *Rouge et noir*. While recuperating from two major operations in 1941 and 1942, Matisse concentrated on a technique he had devised earlier: *papiers découpés* (paper cutouts). *Jazz*, written and illustrated by Matisse, was published in 1947; the plates are stencil reproductions of paper cutouts. In 1948 he began the design for the decoration of Chapelle du Rosaire in Venice, which was completed and consecrated in 1951. The same year a major retrospective of his work was presented at the Museum of Modern Art, New York, which then traveled to Cleveland, Chicago, and San Francisco. In 1952 the Musée Matisse was inaugurated at the artist's birthplace of Le Cateau-Cambrésis. Matisse continued to make large paper cutouts, the last of which was a design for the rose window at Union Church of Pocantico Hills, New York. He died on November 3, 1954, in Nice.

JEAN METZINGER

b. 1883, Nantes, France; d. 1956, Paris

Jean Metzinger was born in Nantes, France, on June 24, 1883. At the age of twenty he moved to Paris to pursue a career as a painter. One of his early friends in Paris was Robert Delaunay. Around 1908 he met the writer Max Jacob, who introduced him to Guillaume Apollinaire and his circle, which included Georges Braque and Pablo Picasso. Picasso was to have a significant influence on Metzinger from this time to about 1923. In 1910 Metzinger exhibited for the first time at the Salon des Indépendants. In 1910 and 1911 he published several articles on contemporary painting and afterward periodically contributed to the literature on modern art. Metzinger was the first to note in print that Picasso and Braque had dismissed traditional perspective and merged multiple views of an object in a single image; his article on this subject appeared in *Pan* (1895–1900; 1910–15) in 1910.

In 1911, with Delaunay, Albert Gleizes, and Fernand Léger, Metzinger participated in the controversial Salle 41 at the Salon des Indépendants, the first formal group exhibition of Cubist painters. His work was represented at the Salon d'Automne in Paris that same year. Metzinger collaborated with Gleizes in 1912 on *Du "cubisme"* (*On "Cubism"*), in which a theoretical foundation for the movement was proposed. During that year he was a founder of the Section d'Or (Golden Section) and exhibited at the Galerie de la Boétie in Paris with other members of the group, including Alexander Archipenko, Roger de La Fresnaye, Gleizes, Juan Gris, Léger, and Louis Marcoussis. In 1913 Metzinger's work was again shown at the Salon d'Automne, and he continued to exhibit in the principal salons of Paris thereafter. This same year he took part in an exhibition at Herwarth Walden's Der Sturm gallery in Berlin and shared a show at the Galerie Berthe Weill in Paris with Gleizes and Léger. In 1916 Metzinger showed with Jean Crotti, Marcel Duchamp, and Gleizes at the Montross Gallery in New York. After military service during World War I, Metzinger returned in 1919 to Paris, where he lived for the remainder of his life. Among his solo exhibitions were those at the Leicester Galleries in London in 1930, the Hanover Gallery in London in 1932, and the Arts Club of Chicago in 1953. The artist died in Paris on November 3, 1956.

AMEDEO MODIGLIANI

b. 1884, Livorno, Italy; d. 1920, Paris

Amedeo Modigliani was born on July 12, 1884, in Livorno, Italy. The serious illnesses from which he suffered during his childhood persisted throughout his life. At age fourteen he began to study painting. He first experimented with sculpture during the summer of 1902 and the following year attended the Reale Istituto di Belle Arti in Venice. Early in 1906 Modigliani went to Paris, where he settled in Montmartre and attended the Académie Colarossi. His early work was influenced by Paul Cézanne, Paul Gauguin, Théophile Alexandre Steinlen, and Henri de Toulouse-Lautrec. In the fall of 1907 he met his first patron, Paul Alexandre, who purchased works from him before World War I. Modigliani exhibited in the Salon d'Automne in 1907 and 1912 and in the Salon des Indépendants in 1908, 1910, and 1911.

In 1909 Modigliani met Constantin Brancusi when both artists were living in Montparnasse. From 1909 to 1914 he concentrated on sculpture, but he also drew and painted to a certain extent. However, the majority of his paintings date from 1916 to 1919. Modigliani's circle of friends first consisted of Max Jacob, Jacques Lipchitz, and the Portuguese painter Amadeo de Souza-Cardoso. Later he associated with Léonard Foujita, Moïse Kisling, Jules Pascin, Osbert and Sacheverell Sitwell, Chaim Soutine, and Maurice Utrillo. His dealers were Paul Guillaume (1914–16) and Léopold Zborowski (by 1917). The only solo show given the artist during his lifetime took place at the Galerie Berthe Weill in December 1917.

In March 1917 Modigliani met Jeanne Hébuterne, who became his companion and model. From March or April 1918 until May 1919, they lived in the south of France, in both Nice and Cagnes. Modigliani died on January 24, 1920, in Paris.

PIET MONDRIAN

b. 1872, Amersfoort, Netherlands;
d. 1944, New York

Piet Mondrian was born Pieter Cornelis Mondriaan Jr. on March 7, 1872, in Amersfoort, Netherlands. He studied at the Rijksakademie van Beeldende Kunsten, Amsterdam, from 1892 to 1897. Until 1908, when he began to take annual trips to Domburg in Zeeland, Mondrian's work was naturalistic—incorporating successive influences of academic landscape and still-life painting, Dutch Impressionism, and Symbolism. In 1909 a major exhibition of his work (with that of Jan Sluijters and Cornelis Spoor) was held at the Stedelijk Museum, Amsterdam, and that same year he joined the Theosophic Society. In 1909 and 1910 he experimented with Pointillism and by 1911 had begun to work in a Cubist mode. After seeing original Cubist works by Georges Braque and Pablo Picasso at the first *Moderne Kunstkring* (*Modern Art Circle*) exhibition in 1911 in Amsterdam, Mondrian decided to move to Paris. There, from 1912 to 1914, he began to develop an independent abstract style.

Mondrian was visiting the Netherlands when World War I broke out and prevented his return to Paris. During the war years in Holland, he further reduced his colors and geometric shapes and formulated his nonobjective Neoplastic style. In 1917 Mondrian became one of the founders of De Stijl (The Style). This group, which included Theo van Doesburg, Bart van der Leck, and Georges Vantongerloo, extended its principles of abstraction and simplification beyond painting and sculpture to architecture and graphic and industrial design. Mondrian's essays on abstract art were published in the periodical *De Stijl* (1917–32). In July 1919 he returned to Paris; there he exhibited with De Stijl in 1923, but withdrew from the group after Van Doesburg reintroduced diagonal elements into his work around 1925. In 1930, Mondrian showed with Cercle et Carré (Circle and Square) and in 1931 joined Abstraction-Création (Abstraction-Creation).

World War II forced Mondrian to move to London in 1938 and then to settle in New York in October 1940. In New York he joined American abstract artists and continued to publish texts on Neoplasticism. His late style evolved significantly in response to the city. In 1942 his first solo show took place at the Valentine Dudensing Gallery, New York. Mondrian died on February 1, 1944, in New York.

EMIL NOLDE

b. 1867, North Schleswig, Nolde, Germany;
d. 1956, Seebüll, West Germany

Emil Nolde was born Emil Hansen on August 7, 1867, in North Schleswig, near Nolde, Germany (now Denmark). He worked as an ornamental carver in furniture factories in Munich, Karlsruhe, and Berlin from 1888 to 1890. After a sojourn in Berlin he moved to Saint Gall, Switzerland, in 1891, where he taught ornamental drawing and modeling at the Industrie und Gewerbemuseum. He studied art with Friedrich Fehr in Munich in 1898 and at the Hölzel-Schule in Dachau in 1899, before visiting Paris that fall to attend the Académie Julian. After stays in Copenhagen, Berlin, and Flensburg, Germany, he settled in 1903 on the island of Alsen.

In 1905, after Nolde returned from a trip to Italy, his first solo show was held at the Galerie Ernst Arnold in Dresden. From 1906 to 1907 he belonged to the Dresden-based group of artists, Die Brücke (The Bridge), who shared his interest in the graphic arts and his admiration for the work of Edvard Munch and Vincent van Gogh. Nolde moved to Dresden in 1907 and developed friendships with Erich Heckel, Ernst Ludwig Kirchner, and Max Pechstein. That same year, the Museum Folkwang in Hagen and the Galerie Commeter in Hamburg presented solo exhibitions of his work. The Berliner Secession, which had rejected Nolde's Expressionist paintings for several years, expelled him in 1910 after he criticized the association's president. In 1912 he participated in the Sonderbund exhibition in Cologne and the second show of Der Blaue Reiter (The Blue Rider) group in Munich. From 1913 to 1914 he traveled across Russia and the Far East to New Guinea. He settled in Berlin in 1915 and spent most winters there until 1940. In 1927 an important traveling retrospective was organized in Dresden, followed the next year by a major solo show at the Kunsthalle Basel. Nolde's paintings were confiscated from German museums by the Nazis in 1937, and he was forbidden to paint, despite his support for the regime. Nolde's first solo show in the United States was held at Curt Valentin's Buchholz Gallery in New York in 1939. The Kestner-Gesellschaft of Hannover presented a retrospective of his work in 1948. Nolde died on April 13, 1956, in Seebüll, West Germany (now Germany), where the Stiftung Seebüll Ada und Emil Nolde (Seebüll Foundation of Ada and Emil Nolde) was formed shortly thereafter.

PABLO PICASSO

b. 1881, Málaga, Spain; d. 1973, Mougins, France

Pablo Ruiz Picasso was born on October 25, 1881, in Málaga, Spain. The son of an academic painter, José Ruiz Blasco, he began to draw at an early age. In 1895 the family moved to Barcelona, and Picasso studied there at La Lonja, the academy of fine arts. His visit to Horta de Ebro from 1898 to 1899 and his association with the group at the café Els quatre gats around 1899 were crucial to his early artistic development. Picasso's first exhibition took place in Barcelona in 1900, and that fall he went to Paris for the first of several stays during the early years of the century. Picasso settled in Paris in April 1904, and his circle of friends soon included Guillaume Apollinaire, Max Jacob, Gertrude and Leo Stein, as well as two dealers, Ambroise Vollard and Berthe Weill.

His style developed from the Blue Period (1901–04) to the Rose Period (1905) to the pivotal work *Les demoiselles d'Avignon* (1907), and the subsequent evolution of Cubism from an Analytic phase (ca. 1908–11) to its Synthetic phase (beginning in 1912–13). Picasso's collaboration on ballet and theatrical productions began in 1916. Soon thereafter, his work was characterized by neoclassicism and a renewed interest in drawing and figural representation. In the 1920s the artist and his wife, Olga (whom he had married in 1918), continued to live in Paris, travel frequently, and spend their summers at the beach. From 1925 to the 1930s Picasso was involved to a certain degree with the Surrealists, and from the fall of 1931 he was especially interested in making sculpture. In 1932, with large exhibitions at the Galerie Georges Petit, Paris, and the Kunsthaus Zürich, and the publication of the first volume of Christian Zervos's catalogue raisonné, Picasso's fame increased markedly.

By 1936 the Spanish Civil War had profoundly affected Picasso, the expression of which culminated in his painting *Guernica* (1937). Picasso's association with the Communist Party began in 1944. From the late 1940s he lived in the south of France. Among the enormous number of exhibitions that were held during the artist's lifetime, those at the Museum of Modern Art, New York, in 1939 and the Musée des arts décoratifs, Paris, in 1955 were most significant. In 1961 the artist married Jacqueline Roque, and they moved to Mougins. There Picasso continued his prolific work in painting, drawing, prints, ceramics, and sculpture until his death on April 8, 1973.

LIUBOV POPOVA

b. 1889, near Moscow; d. 1924, Moscow

Liubov Popova was born on April 24, 1889, near Moscow. After graduating from the Arseniev Gymnasium, she studied art with Stanislav Zhukovsky in 1907 and with Konstantin Yuon and Ivan Dudin in 1908. In the course of travels from 1909 to 1911, she saw Mikhail Vrubel's work in Kiev, ancient Russian churches and icons in Pskov and Novgorod, and early Renaissance art in Italy. In 1912, Popova worked at Tovjer (The Tower), a Moscow studio, with Vladimir Tatlin and other artists. That winter, she visited Paris, where she studied under Henri Le Fauconnier, Jean Metzinger, and André Dunoyer de Segonzac at La Palette. In 1913, Popova returned to Russia, but the following year she journeyed again to France and to Italy, where she gained familiarity with Futurism.

In her work of 1912 to 1915, Popova was concerned with Cubist form and the representation of movement; after 1915, her nonrepresentational style revealed the influence of icon painting. She participated in many exhibitions of advanced art in Russia during this period: the Bubnovyi valet (Jack of Diamonds) group shows of 1914 and 1916 in Moscow; *Tramvai V: Pervaya futuristecheskaya vystavka kartin* (*Tramway V: The First Futurist Exhibition of Paintings*) and *Posledniaia futuristicheskaya vystavka kartin, "0.10" (nul-desat)* (*The Last Futurist Exhibition of Paintings, "0.10" [Zero-Ten]*), both in 1915 in Petrograd (now Saint Petersburg); *Magazin* (*The Store*) in 1916, *Fifth State Exhibition: From Impressionism to Nonobjective Art* in 1918–19, and *Tenth State Exhibition: Non-Objective Creativity and Suprematism* in 1919, all in Moscow. In 1916, Popova joined the Supremus group, which was organized by Kazimir Malevich. She taught at Svobodnye gosudarstvennye khudozhestvennye masterskie (SVOMAS) (Free State Art Schools) and Vysshie gosudarstvennye khudozhestvenno-tekhnicheskie masterskie (VKhuTEMAS) (Higher State Art-Technical Studios) from 1918 onward and worked under Vasily Kandinsky's supervision in the monumental art section at the Institut khudozhestvennoi kultury (INKhUK) (Institute of Artistic Culture) from 1920 to 1923.

The artist participated in the *5 x 5 = 25* exhibition in Moscow in 1921 and in the *Erste russische Kunstausstellung* (*First Russian Art Exhibition*), held under the auspices of the Russian government at the Galerie van Diemen in Berlin in 1922. In 1921, Popova turned away from studio painting to execute utilitarian Productivist art: she designed textiles, dresses, books, porcelain, costumes, and theater sets (the latter for Vsevolod Meierkhold's productions of Fernand Crommelynk's *Velikodushny rogonosets* (*The Magnanimous Cuckold*, 1922), and Serge Tretiakov's *Zemlia dybom* (*Earth in Turmoil*, 1923). Popova died on May 25, 1924, in Moscow.

ENRICO PRAMPOLINI

b. 1894, Modena, Italy; d. 1956, Rome

Enrico Prampolini was born in Modena, Italy, on April 20, 1894. He studied in Lucca, Turin, and Rome, where he briefly attended the Accademia di Belle Arti, studying under Duilio Cambellotti. In 1912 he joined the studio of Giacomo Balla and belonged to a Futurist art collective, through which he met the leaders of the movement, including Umberto Boccioni, Carlo Carrà, and Gino Severini. In 1914 he exhibited with other Futurists at the Galleria Sprovieri in Rome and shortly afterward in Prague.

Many of Prampolini's ideas were a synthesis of those of prominent members of the international avant-garde, but his knowledge and contacts abroad afforded him the role of innovator in Italy. He met Tristan Tzara in Rome in 1916 and took part in the international Dadaist exhibition in Zurich in the same year. His international networks continued to expand as he founded and wrote for a succession of publications, including *Avanscoperta* (1916), *Noi* (1917–25), and *Sic* (1919), and organized exhibitions featuring his work along with other Futurists and international avant-garde artists, such as a 1918 show at the Galleria dell'epoca in Rome along with Giorgio de Chirico, Carrà, and Ardengo Soffici. After extensive travel abroad in the early 1920s and an ongoing exchange of ideas with artists including Alexander Archipenko, Jean Arp, Marc Chagall, Albert Gleizes, and Vasily Kandinsky, Prampolini moved to Paris in 1925. He lived there until 1937, maintaining relations with artistic groups associated with Der Sturm, the Section d'Or (Golden Section), and the Bauhaus. In 1926 he exhibited at the Venice Biennale with the group

Die Abstrakten (The Abstracts), and in 1930 he joined the Parisian group Cercle et Carré (Circle and Square). Shortly afterward he founded the Gruppo 40 (Group 40) and became associated with Abstraction-Création (Abstraction-Creation).

While continuing to paint and exhibit internationally, Prampolini further explored theater, dance, and cinematography. In 1925, he founded the dance company Teatro della Pantomima Futurista, probably as a response to Sergei Diaghilev's Ballets Russes and Rolf de Maré's Ballets Suedois. Prampolini served as the sole set and costume designer. In 1934, he founded the architecturally focused magazine *Stile Futurista* (1933–36); among his building designs were the functional pavilions at Turin (1928) and his pavilion for the fifth Milan Triennale (1933). Toward the end of his life, he expanded into decorative work, including mosaics (for the Museo delle arti popolari, Rome, 1940–41, and for the tenth triennale, Milan, 1954) and stained glass. Prampolini died on June 17, 1956, in Rome.

HENRI ROUSSEAU

b. 1844, Laval, France; d. 1910, Paris

Born May 21, 1844, in Laval, France, Henri Rousseau attended the lycée there until 1860. While working for a lawyer in 1863, Rousseau was charged with petty larceny and joined the army to avoid scandal. He never saw combat and did not travel outside France, but his colleagues' adventures in Mexico inspired him to create legends of his own foreign journeys. Upon his father's death in 1868, Rousseau left the army. The following year he entered the Paris municipal toll-collecting service as a second-class clerk; he was never promoted although he has traditionally been called "Le Douanier" (customs officer). In 1884 Rousseau obtained a permit to sketch in the national museums. He sent two paintings to the Salon des Champs-Elysées in 1885, and from 1886 until his death, he exhibited annually at the Salon des Indépendants.

By 1893 Rousseau retired from the toll service on a small pension and began to paint full-time. The same year the artist met the writer Alfred Jarry, who encouraged him and introduced him into literary circles. In 1899 he wrote a five-act play entitled *La vengeance d'une orpheline russe* (*The Revenge of a Russian Orphan*). A waltz he composed, "Clémence," was published in 1904. Rousseau became friendly with Robert Delaunay by 1906. In 1908 he began to hold musical and family evenings in his studio. Late that year Picasso arranged a banquet in honor of Rousseau, which was attended by Guillaume Apollinaire, Max Jacob, and Marie Laurencin, among others.

By 1909 Rousseau's paintings were acquired by the dealers Joseph Brummer and Ambroise Vollard. His first solo show was arranged in 1909 by Wilhelm Uhde and took place in a furniture shop in the rue Notre-Dame-des-Champs. Rousseau died on September 2, 1910, in Paris. The same year an exhibition of his work in the collection of Max Weber took place at Alfred Stieglitz's gallery 291 in New York. He was given a retrospective at the Salon des Indépendants in 1911.

LUIGI RUSSOLO

b. 1885, Portogruaro, Italy; d. 1947, Cerro di Laveno, Italy

Luigi Russolo was born in Portogruaro, Italy, on April 30, 1885. While his two older brothers graduated from the Milan conservatory, Russolo, after joining his family in Milan in 1901, chose to pursue painting. In 1909 he showed a group of etchings at the Famiglia Artistica (Artistic Family) in Milan, where he met Umberto Boccioni and Carlo Carrà. The following year, after his encounter with Filippo Tommaso Marinetti, Russolo signed both the "Manifesto dei pittori futuristi" ("Manifesto of Futurist Painters") and the "Manifesto tecnico della pittura futurista" ("Technical Manifesto of Futurist Painting"). Afterwards, he participated in all Futurist soirées and exhibitions.

On March 11, 1913, Russolo issued his manifesto "L'arte dei rumori" ("The Art of Noises"), dedicated to fellow Futurist composer Francesco Balilla Pratella. Expanded into book form in 1916, it theorized the inclusion of incidental noise into musical composition. With Ugo Piatti, he later invented the *intonarumori,* noise-emitting machines that allowed for the modification of tone and pitch. In 1913–14, Russolo conducted his first Futurist concerts with numerous *intonarumori.* Audiences in Milan, Genoa, and London reacted with enthusiasm or open hostility. Russolo started to contribute to the magazine *Lacerba* (1913–15), where in 1914 he published his "Grafia enarmonica per gl'intonarumori" (Enharmonic notation for futurist intonarumori), which introduced a new and influential form of musical notation. Later, beginning in 1922, he invented a series of *rumorarmoni*, a kind of harmonium that allowed for the extension of tone and pitch by the simple shift of one register. In 1925 he patented the "enharmonic bow" and later the "enharmonic piano." Russolo appeared in three short Futurist films (now lost), for which he also composed the music.

With the outbreak of the war in 1914, Russolo volunteered, like many of his Futurist friends, in the Battaglione Lombardo Volontari Ciclisti (Lombard Volunteer Cyclists Battalion). After being seriously wounded in December 1917, he spent eighteen months in various hospitals. Due to his opposition to Fascism, Russolo spent most of his time between 1927 and 1932 in Paris. He held his last concert in 1929, presented by Edgard Varèse, at the opening of a Futurist show in Paris at the Galerie 23. In 1931 he moved to Tarragona in Spain, where he studied occult philosophy and then in 1933 returned to Italy, settling in Cerro di Laveno on Lake Maggiore. Russolo published his philosophical investigations *Al di là della materia* (Beyond matter) in 1938. In 1941–42, he took up painting again in a realist style that he called "classic-modern." Russolo died at Cerro di Laveno on February 4, 1947.

EGON SCHIELE

b. 1890, Tulln, Austria; d. 1918, Vienna

Egon Schiele was born on June 12, 1890, in Tulln, Austria. After attending school in Krems and Klosterneuburg, he enrolled in the Akademie der bildenden Künste in Vienna in 1906. There he studied painting and drawing but was frustrated by the school's conservatism. In 1907, he met Gustav Klimt, who encouraged him and influenced his work. Schiele left the Akademie in 1909 and founded the Neukunstgruppe (New Art Group) with other dissatisfied students. Upon Klimt's invitation, Schiele exhibited at the 1909 Vienna Kunstschau, where he encountered the work of Edvard Munch, Jan Toroop, Vincent van Gogh, and others. On the occasion of the first exhibition of the Neukunstgruppe in 1909 at the Piska Salon, Vienna, Schiele met the art critic and writer Arthur Roessler, who befriended him and wrote admiringly of his work. In 1910, he began a long friendship with the collector Heinrich Benesch. By this time, Schiele had developed a personal Expressionist portrait and landscape style and was receiving a number of portrait commissions from the Viennese intelligentsia.

Seeking isolation, Schiele left Vienna in 1911 to live in several small villages; he concentrated increasingly on self-portraits and allegories of life, death, and sex and produced erotic watercolors. In 1912, he was arrested for "immorality" and "seduction;" during his twenty-four-day imprisonment, he executed a number of poignant watercolors and drawings. Schiele participated in various group exhibitions, including those of the Neukunstgruppe in Prague in 1910 and Budapest in 1912; the Sonderbund, Cologne, in 1912; and several Secession shows in Munich, beginning in 1911. In 1913, Galerie Hans Goltz, Munich, mounted Schiele's first solo show. A solo exhibition of his work took place in Paris in 1914. The following year, Schiele married Edith Harms and was drafted into the Austrian army. He painted prolifically and continued to exhibit during his military service. His solo show at the Wien Secession of 1918 brought him critical acclaim and financial success. He died several months later in Vienna, at age 28, on October 31, 1918, a victim of influenza, which had claimed his wife three days earlier.

KURT SCHWITTERS

b. 1887, Hannover, Prussia; d. 1948, Kendal, England

Kurt Schwitters was born Herman Edward Karl Julius Schwitters on June 20, 1887, in Hannover, Prussia (now Germany). He attended the Kunstgewerbeschule in Hannover from 1908 to 1909 and from 1909 to 1914 studied at the Kunstakademie Dresden. After serving as a draftsman in the military in 1917, Schwitters experimented with Cubist and Expressionist styles. In 1918, he made his first collages and in 1919 invented the term "Merz," which he was to apply to all his creative activities: poetry as well as collage and constructions. This year also marked the beginning of his friendships with Jean Arp and Raoul Hausmann. Schwitters's earliest *Merzbilder* (Merz pictures) date from 1919, the year of his first exhibition at Herwarth

Walden's Der Sturm gallery, Berlin, and the first publication of his writings in the periodical *Der Sturm* (1910–32). Schwitters showed at the Société Anonyme in New York in 1920.

With Arp, he attended the Kongress der Konstructivisten in Weimar in 1922. There Schwitters met Theo van Doesburg, whose De Stijl (The Style) principles influenced his work. Schwitters's Dada activities included his *Merz-Matineen* and *Merz-Abende* at which he presented his poetry. From 1923 to 1932, he published the magazine *Merz*. Around 1923, the artist started to make his first *Merzbau*, a fantastic structure he built over a number of years; the *Merzbau* grew to occupy much of his Hannover studio. During this period, he also worked in typography. Schwitters was included in the exhibition *Abstrakte und surrealistische Malerei und Plastik* (*Abstract and Surrealist Painting and Sculpture*) at the Kunsthaus Zürich in 1929. The artist contributed to the Parisian review *Cercle et Carré* (1930). In 1932, he joined the Paris-based Abstraction-Création (Abstraction-Creation) group and wrote for its organ of the same name. He participated in the *Cubism and Abstract Art* and *Fantastic Art, Dada, Surrealism* exhibitions of 1936 at the Museum of Modern Art, New York.

The Nazi regime banned Schwitters's work as *entartete kunst* (degenerate art) in 1937. That year, the artist fled to Lysaker, Norway, where he constructed a second *Merzbau*. After the German invasion of Norway in 1940, Schwitters escaped to Great Britain, where he was interned for over a year. He settled in London following his release, but moved to Little Langdale in the Lake District in 1945. There, helped by a stipend from the Museum of Modern Art, he began work on a third *Merzbau* in 1947. The project was left unfinished when Schwitters died on January 8, 1948, in Kendal, England.

GINO SEVERINI

b. 1883, Cortona, Italy; d. 1966, Paris

Gino Severini was born on April 7, 1883, in Cortona, Italy. He studied at the Scuola Tecnica in Cortona before moving to Rome in 1899. There he attended art classes at the Villa Medici and by 1901 met Umberto Boccioni, who had also recently arrived in Rome and later would be one of the theoreticians of Futurism. Together, Severini and Boccioni visited the studio of Giacomo Balla, where they were introduced to painting with "divided" rather than mixed color. After settling in Paris in November 1906, Severini studied Impressionist painting and met the Neo-Impressionist Paul Signac.

Severini soon came to know most of the Parisian avant-garde, including Georges Braque, Juan Gris, Amedeo Modigliani, and Pablo Picasso; Aurélien Lugné-Poë and his theatrical circle; poets Guillaume Apollinaire, Paul Fort, and Max Jacob; and author Jules Romains. After joining the Futurist movement at the invitation of Filippo Tommaso Marinetti and Boccioni, Severini signed the "Manifesto dei pittori futuristi" ("Manifesto of Futurist Painters") of February 1910 and the "Manifesto tecnico della pittura futurista" ("Technical Manifesto of Futurist Painting") of April 1910, along with Balla, Boccioni, Carlo Carrà, and Luigi Russolo. However, Severini was less attracted to the subject of the machine than his fellow Futurists and frequently chose the form of the dancer to express Futurist theories of dynamism in art.

Severini helped organize the first Futurist exhibition at the Bernheim-Jeune gallery, Paris, in February 1912, and participated in subsequent Futurist shows in Europe and the United States. In 1913, he had solo exhibitions at the Marlborough Gallery, London, and Der Sturm, Berlin. During the Futurist period, Severini acted as an important link between artists in France and Italy. After his last truly Futurist works—a series of paintings on war themes—Severini painted in a Synthetic Cubist mode, and by 1920 he was applying theories of classical balance based on the Section d'Or (Golden Section) to figurative subjects from the traditional commedia dell'arte. He divided his time between Paris and Rome after 1920. He explored fresco and mosaic techniques and executed murals in various mediums in Switzerland, France, and Italy during the 1920s. In the 1950s, he returned to the subjects of his Futurist years: dancers, light, and movement. Throughout his career, Severini published important theoretical essays and books on art. Severini died on February 26, 1966, in Paris.

MARIO SIRONI

b. 1885, Sassari, Italy; d. 1961, Milan

Mario Sironi was born on May 12, 1885 in Sassari, Italy. His father, an engineer, moved the family back to Rome the following year. In 1902 Sironi enrolled in the engineering school at the University of Rome, but soon abandoned his studies. At the Scuola Libera del Nudo, which he began attending in 1903, Sironi met Giacomo Balla, Umberto Boccioni, and Gino Severini. He exhibited at the *Esposizione della Società degli Amatori e Cultori* in 1905, and contributed illustrations to the Socialist journal *L'Avanti della Domenica* (1896–93).

He traveled to Paris in 1906 (where he roomed with Boccioni), Munich in 1908, and Frankfurt in 1910. Suffering from depression, he spent long periods of his youth in seclusion and destroyed most of his early, Divisionist work. At the encouragement of Boccioni, Sironi began to adhere to Futurism late in 1913, participating in the *Prima esposizione libera futurista* (*First Free Futurist Exhibition*) at the Galleria Sprovieri in 1914. By 1915 Sironi had moved to Milan, and, at the invitation of Filippo Tommaso Marinetti, took the place of Ardengo Soffici in the core Futurist group. That same year he signed the Futurist interventionist manifesto "L'orgoglio italiano" ("Italian Pride").

He served at the front with Boccioni, Marinetti, Luigi Russolo, and Antonio Sant'Elia. He continued his work as an illustrator, primarily for the Futurist cultural weekly, *Gli Avvenimenti* (1915–17), in Milan. In 1919 Sironi participated in the *Grande mostra futurista* (*Great Futurist Exhibition*) in Milan, organized by Marinetti as a show of the movement's strength in the immediate postwar period. Yet Sironi was already turning away from the Futurist abstraction in favor of a figurative style and clearly delineated form. That same year he held his first solo show at the Casa d'arte Bragaglia in Rome. In 1920 he signed "Contro tutti i ritorni in pittura" ("Against All Revivals in Painting") with Russolo and other former Futurists: the manifesto argued for a return to pure pictorial values, but without the slavish imitation of the Quattrocento (1400s) primitives represented by Valori plastici (Plastic Values). From 1919 to 1921 he painted his famous series of *paesaggi urbani* (urban landscapes), which transformed Giorgio de Chirico's haunting Italian *piazze d'Italia* (city squares) into contemporary scenes of the Milanese industrial periphery. During the same period he made his reputation as a political commentator in his illustrations for *Le industrie Italiane illustrate* (1917–21).

In 1922 he became one of the founding members of the Sette di novecento (Seven of 1900) in Milan and became the leading exponent of the Novecento italiano (Italian 1900s). Sironi was the chief political caricaturist and illustrator for Mussolini's official press, *Il Popolo d'Italia* (1927–33) and *La Rivista Illustrata del Popolo d'Italia* (1934–39). He was also the leading theorist and practitioner of mural painting and received prominent commissions from the regime. He authored the influential "Manifesto della pittura murale" ("Manifesto of Mural Painting") in 1933. After World War II, he returned to easel painting in a style consistent with the abstract Informel movement. In 1956 he was elected member of the Accademia di San Luca. Sironi died in Milan on August 13, 1961.

VINCENT VAN GOGH

b. 1853, Zundert, Netherlands;
d. 1890, Auvers-sur-Oise, France

Vincent van Gogh was born on March 30, 1853, in Zundert, Netherlands. Beginning in 1869, he worked for a firm of art dealers and at various short-lived jobs. By 1877 Van Gogh had begun religious studies, and from 1878 to 1880 he was an evangelist in the Borinage, a poor mining district in Belgium. While working as an evangelist, he decided to become an artist. Van Gogh admired the work of Honoré Daumier and Jean François Millet; his early subjects were primarily peasants depicted in dark colors. He lived in Brussels and in various parts of the Netherlands before moving to Paris in February 1886.

In Paris he lived with his brother, Theo, and encountered Impressionist and Post-Impressionist painting. Van Gogh worked briefly at Fernand Cormon's atelier, where he met Henri de Toulouse-Lautrec. The artist also met Emile Bernard, Edgar Degas, Paul Gauguin, Camille Pissarro, and Paul Signac at that time. Flowers, portraits, scenes of Montmartre, and a brighter palette replaced his earlier subject matter and tonalities. Van Gogh often worked in Asnières with Bernard and Signac in 1887. In February of the following year he moved to

Arles, where he painted in isolation, depicting the Provençal landscape and people. Gauguin joined him in the fall, and the two artists worked together. In December 1888, after the artists had a falling out, Van Gogh suffered his first mental breakdown. Numerous seizures and intermittent confinements in mental hospitals in Arles, Saint-Rémy, and Auvers-sur-Oise followed from that time until 1890. Nevertheless, he continued to paint. In 1890 Van Gogh was invited to show with Les Vingt (The Twenty) in Brussels, where he sold his first painting. That same year he was represented at the Salon des Indépendants in Paris. Van Gogh shot himself on July 27, 1890, and died on July 29 in Auvers-sur-Oise, France.

PHOTO CREDITS AND COPYRIGHT NOTICES

Archipenko: © 2011 Estate of Alexander Archipenko/Artists Rights Society (ARS), New York; Balla, Carrà, de Chirico, Sironi: © 2011 Artists Rights Society (ARS), New York/SIAE, Rome; Brancusi, Braque, Chagall, Derain, Gleizes, Goncharova, Kandinsky, Kupka, Larionov, Léger, Metzinger, Severini: © 2011 Artists Rights Society (ARS), New York/ADAGP, Paris; Robert and Sonia Delaunay: © L&M Services B.V. Amsterdam; Duchamp: © 2011 Artists Rights Society (ARS), New York/ADAGP, Paris/Succession Marcel Duchamp; Feininger, Jawlensky, Münter, Schwitters: © 2011 Artists Rights Society (ARS), New York/VG Bild-Kunst, Bonn; Kokoschka: © 2011 Fondation Oskar Kokoschka/Artists Rights Society (ARS), New York/ProLitteris, Zurich; Lipchitz: © Estate of Jacques Lipchitz, courtesy Marlborough Gallery, New York; Matisse: © 2011 Succession H. Matisse/Artists Rights Society (ARS), New York; Nolde: © Nolde Stiftung Seebüll; Picasso: © 2011 Estate of Pablo Picasso/Artists Rights Society (ARS), New York

BY FIGURE NUMBER

1: Städtische Galerie im Lembachhaus und Kunstbau München, Munich; 2: © Archives de L'Illustration multimedia; 3: Staatsbibliothek zu Berlin, Stiftung Preussischer Kulturbesitz. Photo: Bildarchiv Preussischer Kulturbesitz/Art Resource, New York; 4: Hilla von Rebay Foundation Archive, M0007, Solomon R. Guggenheim Museum Archives, New York; 5: Courtesy Laura Mattioli; 6: © Roger-Viollet; 7: The Samuel Courtauld Trust, The Courtauld Gallery, London; 8: © Archivio Giovanni Lista, Paris; 9, 14: © Gabriele Münter- und Johannes Eichner-Stiftung, Munich; 10: © Zentralarchiv des internationalen Kunsthandels (ZADIK), Cologne; 11: Bayerische Staatsgemäldesammlungen, Munich, Pinokothek der Moderne. Photo: Bildarchiv Preussischer Kulturbesitz/Art Resource, New York; 12: © The Museum of Modern Art/Licensed by SCALA/Art Resource, New York © 2011 Filippo Tommaso Marinetti/Artists Rights Society (ARS), New York/SIAE, Rome; 13: Hilla von Rebay Foundation Library, Solomon R. Guggenheim Museum, New York; 15, 17: Photo: Bibliothèque nationale de France, Sonia and Robert Delaunay Archives; 16: Digital Image © The Museum of Modern Art/Licensed by SCALA/Art Resource, New York; 18: Deutsches Kunstarchiv, Germanisches Nationalmuseum, Nuremberg, Nachlass Franz Marc, I, A-1; 19: Photo: Kunstmuseum Basel, Martin P. Bühler; 20: Deutsches Kunstarchiv, Germanisches Nationalmuseum, Nuremberg, Nachlass Franz Marc, I, C-10; 21: Staatsbibliothek zu Berlin, Stiftung Preussischer Kulturbesitz, Inv. Hdschr. 125 (Nell Walden), Bl. 42. Photo: Bildarchiv Preussischer Kulturbesitz/Art Resource, New York

BY PAGE NUMBER

24–25: Courtesy Walt Kuhn, Kuhn family papers, and Armory show records, 1859–1978, Archives of American Art, Smithsonian Institution, Washington, D.C.; 60–61: © Gabriele Münter- und Johannes Eichner-Stiftung, Munich; 94–95: Photo: Scala/White Images/Art Resource, New York; 120–21: © The British Library Board, c.108.e.10, p. 5; 158–59: Deutsches Kunstarchiv, Germanisches Nationalmuseum, Nuremberg, Nachlass Franz Marc, I, A-1

ARTIST BIOGRAPHIES

Unless otherwise indicated, the artist biographies are reprinted from Guggenheim.org. Earlier versions of the following biographies first appeared in these publications.

Boccioni: Philip Rylands, ed., *Handbook: The Peggy Guggenheim Collection* (New York: Solomon R. Guggenheim Foundation, 1983); Carrà, Russolo, and Sironi: Laura Mattioli Rossi and Emily Braun, *Masterpieces from the Gianni Mattioli Collection* (New York: Guggenheim Museum, 1997); Derain: *Masterpieces and Master Collectors: Impressionist and Early Modern Paintings from the Hermitage and Guggenheim Museums* (New York: Guggenheim Museum, 2001); Larionov: *From Picasso to Pollock: Classics of Modern Art* (New York: Guggenheim Museum, 2003).